Culture
and
Commitment

Culture
and
Commitment

The Challenge of Today's University

Edward A. Malloy, c.s.c.

NOTRE DAME SESQUICENTENNIAL BOOK

University of Notre Dame Press
Notre Dame   London

Library of Congress Cataloging-in-Publication Data

Malloy, Edward A.
     Culture and commitment : the challenge of today's university
/ Edward A. Malloy.
          p.   cm.
     A collection of the author's significant public addresses given
during his first term as president of Notre Dame.
     "A Notre Dame sesquicentennial book."
     ISBN 0-268-00796-9
     1. Catholic universities and colleges—Philosophy.   2. Cath-
olic universities and colleges—Social aspects.   3. Education,
Higher—Philosophy.   4. Education, Higher—Social aspects.
5. University of Notre Dame.   6. Malloy, Edward A.   I. Title.
LC487.M34   1992
377'.82—dc20   92-50484
                                                                                    CIP

To Theodore M. Hesburgh, C.S.C., 15th President of the University of Notre Dame, mentor, colleague, fellow community member and friend. With thankfulness and high regard.

Contents

Contents

Preface

As president of a university of the prominence of Notre Dame, I regularly—in fact, more often than I can accommodate—am afforded what Theodore Roosevelt termed a "bully pulpit" for sharing my views on a wide variety of issues of current concern.

A person of my calling, of course, needs no introduction to the pulpit, and I have used the opportunities afforded me to discuss various aspects of my vision of higher education, including the value of experiential education through social justice activities, and, of course, the particular mission of Catholic higher education in our highly secularized world.

I have also exploited my training as an ethicist in my speaking and writing, and have reflected at length on the ethical dimensions—both dilemmas and opportunities—of life in the professions.

The fruits of these several labors are here collected.

Acknowledgment

I would like to thank in a special way Dennis Moore who has assisted me in the transcription of oral presentations to various groups and in assisting in the development of a final written form. I would also like to thank Dennis Moore and Carole Roos, from Notre Dame Press, for their assistance in editing the final manuscript.

Introduction

I.

My mother and father grew up in Scranton, Pennsylvania, in the anthracite coal region of northeast Pennsylvania. They were both third generation removed from Ireland. They had a choice to make shortly before I was born; my father did not have a job and the mines were in bad shape. Many people from Pennsylvania were going elsewhere. He had a choice between a revenue agent's job in North Carolina or joining the transit company as a claims adjustor in Washington, D.C. I have always wondered what my life would have been like in the hills of North Carolina. But fortunately, for me anyway, he chose to move to D.C. and I was born in Georgetown University Hospital. At the time of my birth my parents, who had very little money, and my uncles and aunts, who had no money either, were gathered around as the nurse brought me out into the waiting room. My father looked at me and said, "Someday he is going to go to Georgetown." My Uncle John looked at him and said, "No, you are wrong. Someday he is going to go to Notre Dame, and he is going to be president there."

I have two sisters: Joanne, who is one year younger and Mary, who is two and a half years younger. Joanne's job through most of my growing up was to try to keep me humble, especially during the days when I was having athletic success in high school. She would remind me that, even though fans were cheering for me at the gym, most of the world could care less that we had won the game. As I look back on it, that really was an important lesson to be learned, to be able to handle a certain amount of public visibility and acclaim without becoming too impressed with mention of oneself.

Our family took advantage of the amenities of city life, especially those that did not cost anything. We would spend time going to free concerts on the Mall, at the Capitol and the Jefferson Memorial, and at the original Watergate. We would go on trips and picnics to Gettysburg, Harper's Ferry, Manassas, and other similar places in the D.C. area. Very much a part of our life were the famous parades that take place in Washington. There we would marvel at the troops as they marched by and the bands and all the hoopla that went along with being in the capitol city of the nation.

In grade school I had the same teacher, a nun, for three successive years. She took special care to try to convince me and several other of the male students that we had the potential to really do something with our minds, even though we wanted to live a balanced life and enjoy all the things boys do when they are young. Nonetheless, she persuaded us that taking our studies seriously was one of the most important things that we could do; it would give us a position in the future.

Neither of my parents had anything more than a high school education, but they were voracious readers, and so it was a customary thing in my family to have books around. They encouraged me to read whatever was available, and I really believe that was the source of my sense of joy and exhilaration in the act of learning. We would sit around on Sunday evenings and do crossword puzzles together. In fact, we wouldn't go to bed until we finished doing both the Washington Post's and the Washington Star's Sunday crossword puzzles—even if it did involve a little cheating now and then.

When I was in the sixth grade, I tried out for the grade school basketball team, and I had for the first time a sense that I might have some special gifts as a basketball player. I was the only sixth grader chosen for the team, and a couple of eighth graders resented it so much that on the way home from school each day they would grab me and throw me on the ground and sit on me for twenty or thirty minutes. I wouldn't say anything, and eventually they would give up and go away.

When I went to high school, I was fortunate enough to go to a school, Archbishop Carroll, that was just beginning to come into its own as a power in the basketball world. During the course of my time there, our team won fifty-five straight games and were the mythical national champions— probably the best-known team to that point in the history of the city. My graduation year, 1959, was a time of great social change in American society. Under the early and prophetic auspices of Archbishop, later Cardinal, O'Boyle, we were a deliberately and proudly integrated school with about thirty percent black and seventy percent white student population. I think our successful integration happened largely because of the success of our team, which in my senior year, started three black players (including John Thompson, now head coach at Georgetown University) and two whites. The entire city, in fact, identified us as a kind of manifestation of hope for the society at large. I still get letters from people who knew me in those days, from competing coaches and players and those who simply say we're proud of you because you are part of our time and history—and because your school was a class act, a place where harmony and friendship and pulling together, cooperation in a common task, were deeply ingrained values.

When I completed my high school career, Jim Gibbons came out from Notre Dame and recruited me on behalf of Coach Johnny Jordan. I was looking for a school that had an engineering program (I thought I wanted to be a chemical engineer), that was a Catholic school and that was away from the city, that is, away from D.C. I wanted to go away from home because I had an intuition which told me that there was something to be learned by going away—including to better appreciate what I already had. My athletic career at Notre Dame was never as successful as I would have hoped, but it led me to develop some of the other talents that might have lain fallow otherwise. I became involved in various groups, including the social action group CILA (Community of the International Lay Apostolate), which led me to volunteer in Mexico and Peru for three successive summers to work with the poor, to test my own sense of commitment to the needs of the world, to discover by going to another culture what was good and bad about my own, and to bring different kinds of questions into the classroom, something that has motivated me ever since.

While I was in Mexico, I had a searing kind of experience of call, the call from God to be a priest. I can't explain further. It wasn't in a vision, it wasn't something that was describable in normal terms, and perhaps it was prepared for by all the other things that had happened—the people who had influenced me, the many years that I had been an altar boy and all the good priests that I had known, including those at Notre Dame. But I felt a call, and I followed through on it. After graduation, I joined the Congregation of Holy Cross. Everything else that has happened to me, as I see it, is the manifestation of vocation of that call from God to be a priest.

I am privileged to have been chosen the president of Notre Dame, but Notre Dame is more than any one person or any set of people. Notre Dame is a family, a multigenerational family. I can walk out to the Holy Cross community cemetery or I can walk down Notre Dame Avenue to Cedar Grove Cemetery and see the names and recall the stories of the people I have known personally and others that I have only heard about. I can watch the Alumni Reunion groups return each year and see people I know as teachers, friends, students, and individuals in different roles who all have a deep love and loyalty for the University.

Those of us who are Notre Dame students, graduates, and friends always will have a love-hate relationship with the institution. We know firsthand what its flaws are; we know that in measuring up to our rhetoric, we have yet a way to go. But we know too from the friendships we have formed and the opportunities that have opened up to us in this place, that there is a kind of richness here, that there really is a mystique at Notre Dame. We can explain it as the beneficence of Our Lady, Notre Dame, or as the vision of our founder, Fr. Sorin. I don't think there is any one explanation of how it started or how it continues. It is a thing of prayer, of commitment, of loyalty, of dedication. I am honored to have a role within it, particularly carrying on the commitment of the Holy Cross religious community.

II.

If I were asked to describe what is most characteristic about the Holy Cross spirit in higher education, it is that we have been able to attract priests, sisters, and brothers who are able to combine teaching and scholarship with a pastoral presence among students and faculty. This is illustrated by our ongoing presence in the residence halls of Notre Dame. For much of the University's history, Holy Cross religious were the prime adult presence in our dormitories. They served in the roles of rector, assistant rector, and as religious in residence. Depending on the nature and physical layout of the dorm, the style of their ministry varied considerably. Some were Mr. Chips types who were basically avuncular, friendly adult models. Others engaged students through pastoral counselling and participation in the sacrament of penance. Some religious were more severe than others in the enforcement of the rules. But there always have been Holy Cross people who have exercised prudential judgment in tempering what was perhaps an unrealistically high level of expectation for student conduct.

Each generation has its stories to tell. As prefect of religion, Father John O'Hara was famous for his ready availability for confession and distribution of Holy Communion from his room in Sorin Hall. He also composed the religious bulletin, which was a prime vehicle for communicating Catholic values to the student body. John "Pops" Farley was famous for distributing the students' mail, often with comments about its supposed origins, especially female friends. He seems to have been the type of rector who had a winsome way and yet was able to maintain good order. Holy Cross religious in the residence halls have developed a variety of techniques for breaking down barriers in relating to students. Some have looked for common interests in music, cards, sports, or theatre. Others have been ready to invite students to share a meal or to go to some cultural event on or off campus. In recent years, it has not been uncommon for Holy Cross people to visit the homes of Notre Dame families, either with a specific purpose or just in the course of travelling.

Among rectors, one of the most storied gauges of interest in students is the annual effort to learn residents' names quickly, and many Holy Cross rectors have been famous for their ability to master a hall roster of several hundred people in the course of a week or two.

During my twelve years of living in Sorin Hall, I have developed a variety of techniques for getting to know students more personally. Probably the best publicized of these is the tradition called "Monk Hoops," which are regular Monday and Wednesday night basketball competitions. The students gather outside my room around 10:15 at night and we walk over to the Moreau Seminary Gymnasium where we play for about an hour and a half. Most of the time, the crowd numbers sixteen to twenty-two people. We keep two full-court games going with the various teams competing against one another during the night. Except for the walk there and back, it is not a prime occasion for conversation, but it is an enjoyable form of exercise and an ideal way of gaining some insight into the people in the dorm. Of course, they can learn a lot about me in the process as well.

Another way that I get to know students is by inviting freshmen in the dorms to dinner in groups of four or five over the course of the year. Normally, I take them to inexpensive restaurants popular with the students, but sometimes I splurge and we take a step up. If it is early in the year, I use it as a chance for them to describe their backgrounds and the sorts of things we typically discuss with people we are meeting for the first time. If it is later in the year, I try to reach deeper into their lives for the less obvious qualities that may spark new interests among them. I always pay for these meals—in fact, they constitute a fairly good portion of my annual budget—but I have never doubted that it is a valuable way to pay back the hospitality that I have received from so many families over the years. Students who have lived and graduated from Sorin can normally tell me exactly where we went and who was along for the meal, which suggests that it was a noteworthy event of their freshmen years.

In addition to basketball and meals out, I try to talk to as many students as I can individually or in small groups in my room. There is a natural flow of visits over the course of the year, and I try to make the best possible use of it. Still, there are students that I would have almost no contact with if I did not go out of my way to invite them to stop by. I normally employ the resident assistants in the dorm to proffer these invitations and to work out the logistics. The important thing for me is not to be the prime agent of pastoral care in the dorm (since I believe that is the role of the rectors, assistant rectors, and the resident assistants) but to get to know the students and express an interest in them. I know from my experience that I will grow very close to some of them, be familiar with most, and, sadly, will hardly know some at all. But that is rather a common pattern in human relationships.

My one other opportunity to be with the students is as a leader of liturgies. Since becoming president, I have tried to celebrate Mass in all the dormitories over the course of each year. As a result, I celebrate Mass in Sorin only once or twice a semester on Sundays and Tuesday nights. I did more before we had as many priests in the halls as we do now.

Living in a dormitory enhances my availability to the student body in general. I find that the students I teach in my freshman seminar class stop by, and I include a class social event during the semester to strengthen the bonds among them. Students from other dorms stop by spontaneously or because they have a problem or question that they want answered or resolved. Students stop by when their parents are in town, often times to prove they really know me but also to seek advice about how to get things done in the University. I immensely enjoy living in the dorm, because it affords these opportunities to get to know so many really fine people. But it doesn't hurt to have a strategy so that things do not happen simply by chance.

During my first several years in Sorin, I was more directly involved in the supervision of the hall and its people. I served as assistant rector for three and one-half years and as acting rector for a semester. In the course of these assignments, I did pretty much what all residence hall heads do at Notre Dame. I wandered the halls meeting the people in their rooms and maintaining some general order, especially on weekends. I enforced quiet hours and paid particular attention to roommate dynamics and other such things that can be sources of either support or friction. I worked closely with the rector, with the resident assistants and with the hall student government leadership.

After my appointment as an associate provost of the University, I pulled back from most of my formal hall responsibilities for the sake of good order and pastoral care in the hall. The transition was gradual, because for awhile I was one of only two priests in the dorm and, with a new rector, I was the only one who knew the returning students. But since becoming president, I have had to make further adjustments in the allocation of my time and the extent of my presence in the hall. As a matter of principle, I tend never to leave the first floor, whether into the basement or to the second and third floors. My room for the first five years I lived in Sorin was on the second floor where there was no way to avoid passing through student areas on my way in and out of the hall. Living now on the first floor, it is possible for me to avoid becoming immersed in the activity of the hall in ways I don't wish to.

One way I let it be known when I am in my room and available is to put a handwritten welcome sign on my door. For those who live in Sorin, it is an indication that they should feel free to knock at the door and come in. If I am engaged in a serious conversation that I do not want interrupted, I take down the welcome sign and leave the light on in my outer room. Generally, the students have been very respectful of my need for privacy and of the occasional press of University events.

I, of course, live in Sorin twelve months a year, and the schedule is much different during summer when the students are not around. Then and during the semester breaks, I have a lot more time in the evening and on weekends for reading and other projects. In addition, during the school year I have to do a fair amount of traveling, so there are times when I am simply not present. During the fall semester, most of my trips are, at most, overnight; often, I can commute on the University plane in the same day. However, during the spring semester there tend to be many more meetings and conventions that take me away for two or three days at a time. Nonetheless, I have made it a priority to be on campus as often as possible during the school year.

As most parents know from their own experience, the tolerance for various sounds and noises is one of the great gulfs dividing the generations. I am blessed with good hearing, and so I have made it a point to try to provide some buffers to sound in my Sorin quarters. In my present room, I have the chapel on one side, the rector on the other, another priest in residence above me and a resident assistant below me. Along with the two doors I can close to my inner room and to the hallway, this arrangement gives me a fairly quiet room. One of the wisest purchases I ever made is a little electrical device that looks like a small bomb and produces a steady state noise when plugged in. I generally use this in the evening and when there is a social event going on in the dorm. It has the amazing capacity to deaden the noise and promote unbroken sleep. I have gone out of my way to recommend the purchase of this little machine to new people when they move into residence halls.

The bells of Sacred Heart Church in the tower high above my window are a source of some disturbance during the year. I have had a lively exchange of correspondence with Father Dan Jenky, the rector of Sacred Heart, more than once through the years. It is all done in good fun, because after living here all these years, my psyche programs out the sound of the bells on most occasions. The most disturbing of these sounds is the ringing of the funeral toll, but that does not happen very frequently and on most occasions I am participating in the funeral liturgy myself. The freshmen students often complain about the noise of the bells when they first get here, but after awhile they, too, grow accustomed to the distinctive sound of this corner of the campus.

Noise, I must confess, cuts both ways between the generations. I have my own bathroom which is right above a student room, and I have received occasional reminders from the students that, with my late hours, the flushing of the toilet is sometimes disturbing as they try to sleep. I try to be as aware of this problem as I can within the limits of civility and good order in my room.

Compromise and living with occasional mild inconvenience are part and parcel of residence hall life, an element of the learning experience that is a twenty-four hour process in the halls. The lessons learned are valuable, and the inconveniences are compensated many times over by the vitality and community spirit of the halls, which are the stuff of one of Notre Dame's most enduring legacies.

I wouldn't live anywhere else.

PART ONE

The Nature of the Catholic University

Inaugural Address

A university is a bold reminder that the human spirit of curiosity and wonder is irrepressible. In the laboratory, on stage, at the computer terminal, amidst shelves full of books, wherever learners gather, a university sparkles and generates an energy that can captivate and enthrall. Clearly its work touches the core of human meaning and purpose.

In addition to the intrinsic value of the efforts of professors and students, a university also serves the broader society of which it is a part. It requires high levels of expenditure and sufficient freedom to concentrate on its primary mission. At any given moment it is subject to legislation, litigation, and external pressures from many sources. Surely a university cannot function well unless it musters the support, philosophical and financial, of the constituencies that have called it into being. Today this entails accreditation and periodic review, the establishment and funding of endowments, and the structuring of the collective effort for maximum effectiveness.

At Notre Dame and throughout higher education, one of the great challenges is to find the proper balance between the demands of teaching and the demands of research. Teaching and research are indispensably linked together in a university setting. Yet each institution charts its own course and fosters a climate which may give priority to one or the other.

Teaching is best seen as a highly personal interaction between professor and students. It is not acceptable at Notre Dame to engage in it in a perfunctory or indifferent fashion. Our students deserve a total commitment of their mentors to providing a lively and stimulating educational environment. In the full sense of the term, teaching is a 'vocation,' a 'calling'. It is a privilege to be entrusted by society with a responsibility for the intellectual, aesthetic, and moral growth of the next generation.

Research, on the other hand, is a rather solitary and unpredictable pursuit. It increasingly requires sophisticated instrumentation, high quality libraries and computing facilities, and external support for both researchers and graduate students. It is necessarily expensive and ever pressed by new problems and unpredictable lines of exploration. It is in this area of its academic life that Notre Dame has made the greatest strides in the last two decades under the leadership of Provosts James Burtchaell, C.S.C., and Timothy O'Meara. There is no turning back. We must enthusiastically embrace our potential as a major research institution and we must define those areas of scholarly pursuit where we are especially well suited to make a lasting contribution. In a number of instances, it will be through our institutes and centers that our research excellence will be most visible to the broader academic community.

Teaching and research both count at Notre Dame. Our standards are high but so are the rewards.

Notre Dame is a 'Catholic' university. Its distinctiveness as a religious institution is its greatest strength.

In 1967, when the University moved from ownership by the Indiana Province of the Congregation of Holy Cross to a Lay Board of Control, the Statutes of the University specified that the "essential character of the University as a Catholic institution of higher learning shall at all times be maintained, it being the stated intention and desire of the present Fellows of the University that the University shall retain in perpetuity its identity as such an institution." At that same time, special encouragement was provided for a continuing and critical role for the members of the Congregation of Holy Cross in the intellectual, pastoral, and administrative functions of the University.

In an earlier era, the Catholicity of Notre Dame could simply be presumed, seemingly guaranteed by its ownership by a religious community, by the force of its history, and by the overwhelmingly Catholic background of its students and staff. However, new circumstances have arisen, and, to some, the rationale for Notre Dame's religious distinctiveness is not readily apparent.

In the face of these misgivings, I want to assert with deep conviction that the Catholicity of Notre Dame is both a gift and a responsibility. To me, there is nothing inherently incompatible between academic excellence and the life of faithful discipleship. The Church of Thomas Aquinas and Bonaventure, of Teresa of Avila and John of the Cross, of Dante, Michelangelo, Gerard Manley Hopkins, Flannery O'Connor, and Walker Percy can surely boast that it is at home with the things of the mind and heart.

Notre Dame will continue self-consciously and proudly to proclaim itself to be a Catholic university. In one sense, this distinguishes it from secular and nondenominational colleges and universities with different missions. More pointedly, the Catholic identity builds on the historical connection to the Roman Catholic Church and its cultivation of the great transcendental values of truth, beauty, and goodness. It presupposes that a life given over to learning and scholarship can be a valid route to God.

In another sense, Notre Dame's Catholic character is a call to be a community, a kind of external family where individuals from all backgrounds and of every faith can both feel at home and be prized for the special contributions that they make. It is a call to cultivate a spirit of honest and open exchange, always in a valuing context.

Notre Dame rightly continues to maintain a core curriculum, including required courses in philosophy and theology. It provides numerous opportunities for worship, prayerful reflection, and social service. Furthermore, it makes special demands on its students and those responsible for their education. This includes a proper sense of responsibility for one's conduct and for those matters which affect the common good. In all of these ways, it tries to attend to the whole person—intellectual, moral, and spiritual.

Notre Dame is a Catholic university. It preserves the heritage of Father Edward Sorin, C.S.C., its founder, with confidence and trust.

Notre Dame is also a community. It must therefore attend with care and compassion to the well-being of all its members.

There has always been a special feel about this place. Much of its sense of community is forged initially in the residential life of the students, where each dorm has its own unique traditions and characteristic spirit.

The mystique of Notre Dame, its pervasive spirit of togetherness, is an intangible reality. At its best, it takes the form of a priority for persons, a concern for the inner world of colleagues and companions. It is the breeding ground of lifelong friendships and uncommon loyalty to the institution as a source of continuing nurturance. It is manifest most tangibly in times of celebration or crisis, the turning points of life. The creation of community at Notre Dame is a family-like thing, the wish that there be no strangers here.

Yet, like all families, we also suffer our misunderstandings and disputes. At times, we neglect the needful in our midst, we stereotype minorities, and we treat with disdain those flauntingly different. We regretfully allow gender or race or status and rank to fracture our commonality and drive us apart. In recognition of this inconsistency and harm, we ever need to acknowledge our failure and move to reform our common life.

Notre Dame is and must be a community. For only thus can it be true to its call.

Notre Dame has a mission of service to society and the Church. This mission is primarily intellectual and academic, but it builds upon concrete experience and overflows from theory into committed practice.

There are presently 235 colleges and universities in the system of Catholic higher education in the United States. This is an impressive reservoir of talent, energy, and research capacity. Among these institutions, Notre Dame has, I think, its own special role to play in the collective outreach to society and the Church.

Society has a right to expect from us a continual stream of thoughtful and well-trained men and women who can exercise leadership in the workplace, in the social world, and in all of those private and public organizations and agencies that promote the common good. These graduates should be literate and cultured, appreciative of the humane uses as well as the limits of science and technology, able to criticize the status quo yet knowledgeable of history and the proper function of law. As the quality of research and scholarship at Notre Dame progressively improves, we stand as a great resource for society much the same as other major universities, private and public.

In a related way, the Church should find in us a conducive environment to do its thinking. What better place to explore the mysteries of the life of faith, to preserve and interpret the testimony of Scripture and theological tradition, and to ponder the power of prayer and sacrament? We have among us exegetes and ethicists, liturgists and church historians. There is also the ongoing witness of practicing Christians, married and single, grappling to make sense of sin and forgiveness, to practice in daily terms the virtuous triad of faith, hope, and love, and to be responsible citizens in a complex, stressful world.

As has always been the case, the best theory is forged in the crucible of experience. We at Notre Dame have structured opportunities for concrete involvement in the social, political, and ecclesial orders. Through internships and summer study, through foreign study centers, and through the umbrella of organizations affiliated with the Center for Social Concerns, we provoke the awareness of faculty and students alike. The mission of service begins in the activity of students and faculty in shelters for the homeless, in tutoring projects, and in neighborhood renovation. But their experience of the plaintive cry of the poor and disheartened returns to the classroom and to the research project to seek a better and more just way.

In the commitment to justice and peace, in efforts at spiritual and moral renewal, Notre Dame has a mission to society and the Church.

Notre Dame is an open forum where diverse viewpoints can be freely and critically discussed. A unique opportunity presently exists to focus on the moral and ethical dimensions of contemporary life.

The American system of constitutional government provides protection for certain freedoms deemed essential for the well-being of its citizens. Among these protected rights are freedom of speech and freedom of religious practice. In the sphere of higher education, a deeply rooted tradition has developed of academic freedom with its correlative system of tenure for faculty.

At Notre Dame the "Academic Articles" of *The Faculty Handbook* specify explicitly that freedom of inquiry and freedom of expression are to be safeguarded. Each category of participant in the University community has both rights and obligations under this formulation. The freedom to teach and to learn, to publish and to speak, are essential components of this notion of academic freedom.

There are some risks associated with both academic freedom and faculty tenure. They can be the pretext for demagoguery, ideological carping, or a lack of accountability for ongoing preparation and performance. Particularly in a religiously affiliated institution, there can be fear that the authentic teaching of the Church will be misrepresented or subject to unsympathetic critique.

Yet it is crucial to remind all observers of this unique system of higher education in America that the life of learning and scholarship has flourished here. Catholic colleges and universities have found that a plurality of perspectives and methodologies enriches the search for more adequate ways of articulating the truth about the natural order, the human condition, or the divinity. Conflict, controversy, and bracing debate are often the precondition for resolution of the more harrowing and perplexing issues of the day.

Notre Dame's institutional commitment to the principle of academic freedom well situates us to focus on the moral (descriptive) and the ethical (prescriptive) dimensions of contemporary life. Here we can explicitly make reference to the central values of the Judaeo-Christian tradition—respect for life in all its forms, compassion for the neighbor in need, peacemaking, and the inviolability of marriage and family life. But we can do more than simply exhort. We can also explore the full meaning of ethical notions like personal integrity and corporate responsibility. Together we can amicably disagree about nuclear deterrence and test tube babies, economic justice and global pollution. Because we believe that the truth will prevail in a context of honest debate and good-willed searching, we can avoid forming into hostile camps or settling into the quicksand of utter moral relativism.

Notre Dame must remain an open forum where diverse viewpoints can be freely and critically discussed.

The Faith Mission of Catholic Higher Education

*I*n the reading from the Book of Numbers, we find the Jewish people grown impatient with their desert journey. They had risked everything in their quest for the Promised Land, and now they wanted some guarantee of security and continuity of place. They yearned for a permanent home (maybe even one with windows in every room). In frustration, they grumbled against God and their leader Moses. Because of their recalcitrance, God both punishes them (with a plague of serpents) and offers them relief (through the bronze serpent mounted on a pole, lifted up for all to see).

From the vantage point of the later Christian community, this healing emblem was seen as a foreshadowing of the 'lifting up' of Jesus of Nazareth on the Cross. The author of John's Gospel employs this vertical image to stress the irony of the situation. A practice of criminal punishment intended to be disgraceful and censorious has become, in fact, an exaltation. Expressed in other terms, the Suffering Servant, the Paschal Lamb, has broken the shackles of space and time and opened up the prospect of eternal life.

In the final text, the great christological hymn from Paul's letter to the Phillippians, God empties himself in Jesus, becoming like a slave in sharing the fullness of the human condition. Yet his death on a cross is revealed to be, not a moral surd, a futile gesture by a misguided religious fanatic, but rather an act of ultimate obedience. Thus he is entitled to be called "Lord" for he is above every power, even the scourge of death.

What are we to make of this spiritual conundrum, this perplexing claim? In what sense is the Cross a triumph? What practical import does the acceptance of this reality have for life in contemporary society? In what ways should it influence the kind of education that takes place at Notre Dame?

In its most fundamental sense a Catholic university should be the kind of institution where such questions can be attended to with seriousness, reverence, and mutual respect. In response to such core mysteries of the cosmic order, there is no easy route to insight and understanding.

Even if we begin at the descriptive level with the problem of human suffering, it is difficult to make progress in our comprehension. How overwhelming is the quotient of pain! Our minds resist too detailed a recall of the horrors of the past and present. We have known barbarities enough—pirates and marauders, gulags and torture chambers, inquisitions and pogroms of all kinds. Yet artists and poets, historians, philosophers and theologians continue to engage our imaginations, often in spite of ourselves, so that we might share in the lament of Job over the suffering of the innocent. Picasso's stark images in "Guernica"; Doctor Rioux ministering in the plague-infested city of Oran; Wiesel's boyhood memories of Nazi brutalization; the haunting society of post-nuclear devastation in *A Canticle for Liebowitz*—these and thousands of other images enable us to *remember* and thus to confront, if only indirectly, the problem for which the Cross is the ultimate symbol.

But what about the triumph—what remedy would we propose for the evils and injustices of our lives in the present?

How can we move from description and analysis to prescription and amelioration? For the Christian, there is no final solution within human history. Yet there are partial answers and some are far preferable to others. There is no real excuse for sloth or indifference. There is much that an academic community can contribute with its wealth of talent and resources. We can help clarify the values at stake in a given situation. We can appraise alternate courses of action, participate in policy formulation, and learn from the mistakes of the past. We can cultivate beauty in its many modes, highlight proper practices of physical and mental health, and resist threats to the well-being of the young and the innocent. In this sense, a university should be interested in *results*, in more than theoretical formulations and spontaneous curiosity. It should be a focusing agency, a community of common concern where the great issues are addressed with openness and enthusiasm. We must remain a people of hope who avoid the retreat into dispassionate objectivity. This is our most obvious contribution to the Triumph of the Cross.

It is not only in its relationship to the broader society that a university such as this has a contribution to make in preserving a climate of hope in the world. It also teaches by the way it organizes its internal life and by the way its members participate in their given professions.

A Catholic university must be a *hospitable environment* where the life of the mind and the urgings of the heart are taken seriously. Both those who stand within the community of faith and those who come as fellow-searchers for the ultimate source of life and human meaning should find welcome here. There should be no enemies or aliens in a university, a truly Catholic university. On the one hand, Christian scholars should openly and unabashedly draw upon their particular sources of truth and inspiration—the Scriptures, the theological tradition, the Christian liturgy, the great spiritual writers—as well as the best of contemporary discussion, whatever its source. On the other hand, other traditions should be studied and appreciated in their own terms. Points of convergence and agreement should be pursued and disagreements acknowledged honestly. A truly Catholic university, which is simultaneously faithful to its distinctive legacy and promotes an open forum for contrary points of view, will require continual attention to the kind of atmosphere that prevails among faculty and students.

Representing a variety of backgrounds and a diversity of expertise, faculty members should aspire to become people of intellectual and moral virtue, fitting representatives of the profession of teacher-scholar. Three qualities seem especially appropriate.

First, let us be *humane* in our dealings with one another and with our students. Let us prove that it is possible to combine critical judgment with a gentleness of spirit. Back-biting, pettiness, and rivalry are the bane of any community and they are surely irreconcilable with scholarly cooperation and pedagogical credibility.

Secondly, let us be *courageous* in our confrontation with falsehood and pomposity. There is normally little reward for those who remind society of its inconsistencies, call the president or mayor to task, or refuse to overlook a colleague's irresponsibility. Few among us really yearn to be prophets or desire to suffer social stigma as an unpopular critic. Nevertheless, courageous confrontation is a role that is essential for societal well-being. We need voices to protest against the taking of life at its various stages, to defend the rights of classes of people deprived of legitimate expression and remuneration, and to assure the freedom of religious assembly.

Finally, let us be *humble* in the recognition of our personal limitations and the biases which distort our perception of reality. Perhaps the greatest temptation of the professional academic is to pretend to a greater level of competence or a more extensive range of knowledge than he or she could ever possess. We each tap into a great legacy of research, creativity, and scholarship produced by our predecessors. And after we are gone, God willing, the effort will continue.

We are part of a grand endeavor, but only a part. May our recognition of our *relative* importance in the great scheme of things qualify our claims and make us perpetual learners.

Humaneness, courage, and humility are fitting virtues for the teacher-scholar in a place like Notre Dame. Just as a welcoming environment can bring out the best in those who come here, so the personal dedication of the individual faculty can manifest in some sense the hope that comes with the triumph of the Cross.

For the Christian, the Cross stands at the boundary line between senselessness and meaning. It is the symbol of the seeming irrationality of human suffering and of the true deep desire of the human heart for some better, cosmic solution. We at Notre Dame need each other if we would proclaim the Lordship of Christ and explore with sensitivity all of the ramifications of that message. While not all share our Christian convictions, all can take comfort from our commitment to human betterment.

Revise and Dissent

I regard Catholic higher education in this country as both a great American success story and one of the paramount achievements in the history of the church.

Why such a pronouncement now? First, because it is true; second, we should be reminded of it by the recent bicentennial year of American Catholic higher education. In 1789 Georgetown University became the nation's first Catholic institution of higher education; today, more than 200 Catholic colleges and universities dot this country's educational landscape—institutions that have evolved from cultural shelters for the children of immigrants into true centers of scholarship and teaching.

Despite its achievements, Catholic higher education has often been viewed in recent years through the narrow lens of controversy—generated by the Curran case, the proposed Vatican document on higher education, and the presence of pockets of criticism in the Catholic and secular press. I understand the attraction of controversy and the fascination it exerts, but a focus on controversy, like a telephoto lens, eliminates the background and distorts the perspective of events. As a result, context gets lost.

Two examples occurred within weeks of each other last spring: first, when members of the American hierarchy journeyed to the Vatican for a special meeting with the pope and then, shortly afterwards, when Catholic educators, I among them, followed in the bishops' wake to discuss the proposed document on Catholic higher education. In both instances, pre-meeting speculation was suffused with the smell of battle. Then, when both meetings turned out to be encouragingly open, frank and hopeful—when, that is, the anticipated clashes did not develop—interest quickly sagged.

Because I believe Catholic educators must be actively and consistently involved in any disagreement concerning their role in the church or society, I felt a special sense of responsibility when I was chosen to be one of the American delegates to this Vatican meeting, and again when I was elected to serve on the commission named to consult in the preparation of the latest revision of the higher education document. One area of perennial concern between Catholic universities and the church is the division of labor, so to speak, between the bishops—the church's traditional teachers and preservers of the faith—and its scholars, both lay and religious. This concern is not just in theology but in every university discipline. This relationship has a history that ranges across two millennia of Christian existence.

In the best of times, the interaction of bishops and scholars is harmonious and mutually supportive; some bishops, like Saint Augustine of Hippo, have had a decisive influence on theological development. But even during periods of misunderstanding, the ferment is a sign that the church truly is being forced to come to grips with some matter of faith or practice that ultimately must be resolved.

Large issues do not lend themselves to final solutions. Whenever there is change in society or the church—and when is there not?—the last balance struck is disturbed anew and the issue joined again. As far as teaching is concerned, a dual tension has been clearly in evidence from the earliest days. On the one hand, there is the tension created by differing interpretations of the legacy of Christ: Who is empowered to interpret Scripture and tradition? How far may one stretch the limits of interpretation? And who is to adjudicate when disagreements arise? At its worst, this tension has divided the church, sometimes briefly, at other times with long-lasting divisions.

The sensitivity of the theologian's position in the church is obvious. The scholars work—to seek to recall and record the legacy of Christian theory and practice in all its subtleties and permutations, and to attempt the constant reformulation of this tradition in the light of contemporary understanding— is certain to collide at times with perceptions of established teaching. He or she must face a range of questions growing from trends in contemporary intellectual life, from the prevalence of positivist methodologies purportedly based on modern science to the debunking or reductionist tendency found in so much social-scientific literature. The creeping influence of such trends seems to call into radical doubt the ability of the church to teach with both truth and relevance. At the same time, the work of the scholar in tackling these currents of thought may seem to run counter to the teaching of the church. What then?

Compounding these tensions is the tendency of some to believe—not without semi-official encouragement—that the church has never changed and can never change in any significant detail. The fact is, of course, that the church, like any living body, has never ceased to change. In the early letters of Paul, the picture of the infant Christian community with its primitive organizational structure and general unsettledness stands in contrast to the more established churches presumed in the pastoral epistles and the Gospel of John. The first-century Council of Jerusalem, which debated the imposition of Jewish cultic practices on Gentile converts, is a reminder that even Peter and Paul were not immune to the need to make hard choices in a fast-changing world.

Looking back over the span of history, it is evident that the church has never displayed complete conformity; its teachings have been reformed and refashioned over time. Difference, disagreement, accommodation and change—all elemental traits of the human condition—have been with us from the beginning.

Some change has come relatively painlessly, much has not. At various times the church has seen one branch opposing another, one bishop opposing another, even one saint opposing another. The Nicene Creed, which we revere today as one of the great orthodox expressions of faith, emerged from a council held in a period of confrontation so intense that the church appeared likely to be torn into hostile camps.

Again during the High Middle Ages, a period often popularly characterized as the "Golden Era of Catholicism," tensions were manifest. For example, Saint Thomas Aquinas, subsequently proclaimed a Father of the Church, was the target of severe criticism for his appropriation of Greek philosophy, particularly his effort to mingle the mind and methods of the pagan Aristotle with the tenets of faith. At one point, troops had to be called onto the campus of the University of Paris to protect him from those who were protesting his teaching.

For us, Aquinas is the symbol of the flowering of the great European Catholic universities, the period of which Cardinal Newman wrote: "When was there ever a more curious, more meddling, bolder, keener, more penetrating, more rationalistic exercise of the reason than at that time? What class of question did that subtle, metaphysical spirit not scrutinize? What premise was allowed without examination? What principle was not traced to its first origin, and exhibited in its most naked shape? What whole was not analyzed?"

All this is true. In fact, that explosion of learning—of research and instruction—continues to serve as the model for Catholic higher education today. But at the same time that this great flowering was taking place, such classic texts as Aristotle's *Natural Philosophy and Metaphysics* remained officially under interdict. Those prohibitions were largely ignored in the universities, and certainly by Aquinas, but the attitude of fear and mistrust they represented prompted widespread attacks on Thomism.

Examples of such conflicts can be found in every century. Many unresolved issues burst forth at the time of the Protestant Reformation, with Catholics poised against Lutherans, Lutherans against Calvinists, and Calvinists against Anabaptists. The sacramental system, papal and episcopal authority, veneration of the saints and the Blessed Mother, the popular reading of Scripture—these and many other theological topics were debated not only in the academy and from the pulpit but, unfortunately, also on the fields of war.

The church of the apostles and martyrs, the church of missionary zeal and the great promoter of the arts also has been the source of jaundiced opposition to scientific exploration and callous participation in the unjust structures of privilege. It has in periods of darkness justified the Crusades, the arbitrary inflicting of torture, the institution of slavery, and the subordination of women. Honesty requires that we acknowledge both the best and worst of this sometimes rocky journey to the Kingdom we seek.

Writing for *The Critic* about this troubling history of, as he calls it, "diversity in the Church," John Tracy Ellis said, ". . . I know of few more helpful guidelines in this oftentimes tortuous matter than the lives of the Church's most original and creative minds, men and women who were likewise endowed with marked personal sanctity. I think, for example, of a Saint Teresa of Avila, threatened by the Inquisition because of her innovations regarding the contemplative life, yet pushing on with her reform of the Carmelites while ever attentive to the will of her superiors."

Ellis drew one of the critical lessons of the tumultuous history of the church. "History cannot resolve contemporary problems," he wrote, "but it can shed light on them from previous experience. If, then, we of this postconciliar age feel anxious, uncertain, and at times perhaps discouraged by the divisiveness that obtains within our ranks as a Catholic community, we should remember that virtually every postconciliar period that followed the church's twenty-one ecumenical councils was marked by a similar aftermath.

Newman's profound historical sense bore witness to this fact, when as a sequel to Vatican Council 1, its decrees became the subject of sharp and often bitter dissension both within and without the Catholic community. In the midst of this heated controversy the great Oratorian remarked: 'One of the incidental disadvantages of a General Council is that it throws individual units through the Church into confusion and sets them at variance . . . .' "

And so it is in this, our postconciliar age. Nevertheless, I believe that the church possesses the resources to change and to prevail in its mission to the world. My belief is based first of all on the abiding presence of the Holy Spirit, but it is reinforced by the experiences of personal conversion and social reform, two dynamics that have been with the church since the beginning.

Resistance to change springs from certain recognizable traits in us all—a genuine reverence and devotion for the traditional and familiar modes of Christian conviction and expression; a collateral mistrust of the modern, the secular, and the faddish; and a difficulty in absorbing emotionally the loss of devotions, forms of worship, and catechetical formulas that were experienced in one's youth. Such loss can make it seem as if the inner core of the self has been rendered suddenly vulnerable—or, worse, indifferent to God's presence and call.

While none of us wants to capitulate to the alien pressures of contemporary life or to give up our rooting in the heart of the Gospel, some in the church adamantly resist even the appearance of change. Newman provided the best description of these self-appointed guardians: "In spite of the testimony of history the other way, they think the Church has no other method of putting down error than the arm of force, or the prohibition of inquiry." And so we hear of letter-writing campaigns to the bishops and to the Vatican (much easier to organize in the era of the word processor), sounding the alarm and giving the impression that the sky is falling in the American church. Without doubt, this hostility to diversity, this insistence that change is inimical to the church, intensifies debate over the issues we face today, increasing suspicion and rendering our disagreements more confrontational than they need be.

These alarms also bring into play another tension within the church—the significant cultural differences between American and European society. Speaking at the meeting of the American bishops with Pope John Paul last March, Archbishop John May of Saint Louis summarized these differences when he said that Americans are no more inclined to accept the divine right of bishops than to accept the divine right of kings.

Again, history tells the tale. In Europe, the often-turbulent history of the church and the always-turbulent history of kingdoms and nations have been inextricably intertwined. Europe saw the rise and fall of Christendom, from Constantine and Charlemagne to the development of nation-states and the horror of successive world wars. The Renaissance and the Enlightenment, the wars of religion and the wars of revolution, the clash of feudal society with emerging and unrestrained capitalism—all these social forces profoundly affected the life and well-being of the church.

It is not surprising that many sources of bitterness and confusion remain. Europe has seen at various times hostility to the church from the working class, the gentry, and those who despise religion out of cultural or intellectual bias. The Continent has experienced pervasive anticlericalism, hostile secret societies, and intense persecutions.

Our own history is different. Not that Catholics always have been welcome here—recall the nativists and the Know-Nothings and the Ku Klux Klan—yet there is an essential difference. In Europe, the church often has felt, with historical justification, that any government which does not institutionalize religion will be its enemy. Here, by contrast, our hope and protection from the beginning has been the guaranteed impartiality of the government—the twin constitutional guarantees of individual religious freedom and the strict separation of church and state.

These guarantees inspired America's first archbishop, John Carroll, to insist that the American church seek always to engage rather than confront society, to be a full and willing participant in the civic community. Notre Dame's founder, Father Edward Sorin, shared Carroll's patriotism and vision of Catholic renewal.

For Sorin and the pioneers in other religious communities, the key to realizing the church's opportunities in America was the preparation of American Catholics to pursue their personal opportunities in society—another notion very different from the traditional European concept. Here, education was not to be the preserve of an elite but an extension of the belief that every person possesses the inalienable right to become whatever he or she is capable of becoming. It is not surprising, then, that Catholic colleges and universities— Notre Dame included—were not in their early incarnations intellectually distinguished; they were not intended to be. Rather, they were intended to—and did—take the sons (and daughters, though unfortunately to a lesser degree) of immigrants and make of them priests and lawyers, merchants and politicians, whose own sons and daughters could aspire to equal or greater accomplishments.

In short, our colleges and universities accomplished magnificently what they set out to do, for as more and more opportunities opened to American Catholics, more and more American Catholics were prepared to seize them.

At the same time, American Catholic higher education faithfully discharged its mission as a transmitter of the faith. The growth in size and influence of the American Catholic Church was not just a matter of numbers, it was a function of devotion, vocations, philanthropy, and the strength of parish life. In the major cities of America, Catholic parishes often had an influence in their neighborhoods far disproportionate to the size of their congregations. And prominent in those parishes were the graduates of Catholic colleges and universities.

The success of American Catholic higher education brought with it a new challenge. As the American Catholic community has grown more affluent, more influential, and more sophisticated, Catholic colleges and universities have been called upon to place themselves among the nation's and the world's foremost institutions of teaching and scholarship—in other words, to revive the heritage of the great medieval universities. Certainly, we at Notre Dame are pursuing this mission with relish—as are others throughout Catholic higher education. As we do so, however, we inevitably leave ourselves open to the charge that we are abandoning tradition, secularizing our institutions and, particularly with respect to theology, threatening the teaching authority of the church.

The increased public prominence of theologians serves as the lightning rod for such charges. In sharp contrast with the past, when theological research and speculation was shared only among a small circle of intellectuals, today new interpretations of tradition may become the subject of cover stories in national news magazines. This capacity for newsmaking imposes a new responsibility on theologians—the responsibility always to make clear the difference between the core truths of Christian faith and the philosophical and theological categories employed to explicate them; between the integral components of Christian teaching and those issues and problems that still elude ready solution; between the public faith of the community and the experience and speculation of the individual believer.

But the maturing intellectual quality of Catholic higher education—in theology and in all disciplines—also requires mature support from the church at large. The essence of scholarship is to investigate, to propose, and to test, which means to err as well as to discover. "There are no shortcuts to knowledge," Newman wrote, "nor does the road to it always lie in the direction in which it terminates, nor are we able to see the end on starting. It may often seem to be diverging from a goal into which it will soon run without effort, if we are but patient and resolute in following it out."

Happily, we in education for the most part already enjoy the support we seek. Last June, the National Conference of Catholic Bishops approved, by a vote of 214 to 9, a new document on the relationship between theologians and bishops. It cites the good cooperation between American bishops and theologians, encourages informal dialogue as a means to further that cooperation, and stresses flexibility and collaboration in resolving doctrinal disputes.

Archbishop May, addressing the annual meeting last June of the Catholic Theological Society of America, said, "Very bluntly, I think the church in the United States suffers from too many anxious, warning voices that would divide the bishops against the theologians. . . . I stress how imperative it is for you [theologians] to realize that you have the strong and grateful support of us bishops for your work in dealing with problems of enormous complexity and difficulty—problems which bear crucially upon the belief and practice of the church."

Archbishop May's clear and unequivocal support for our educational mission echoes that of his fellow archbishop, Rembert Weakland of Milwaukee. In the May 27 issue of *America*, Monsignor Frederick McManus, himself a professor of canon law at Catholic University of America, quoted Weakland's 1985 defense of academic freedom at Marquette University: "We all must learn in a free society to discern right from wrong, truth from falsehood. . . . Of course, there are risks, but there are just as many risks in denying to teachers the freedom that has been part of our academic heritage for centuries. I, too, hope that teachers always clearly distinguish what is official church teaching from their own views. But to apply to a Catholic university any tactics that would resemble those of a totalitarian state and that would deprive it of its academic freedom would indeed be an even more dangerous process in the long run."

To the archbishop's statement, McManus appended his own suggestion—"in the Catholic community at large, perhaps the answer is more faith and less fear"—which recalls yet another admonition of the great Newman: "I say, then, he who believes Revelation with that absolute faith which is the prerogative of a Catholic, is not the nervous creature who startles at every sound and is fluttered by every strange or novel appearance which meets his eyes."

What we require today in Catholic higher education is no more than Aquinas required at the dawning of the first great age of Catholic universities, no more than Newman prescribed as essential to the idea of the university. Monsignor McManus reminds us of the seventeenth-century maxim, "Let (Truth) and Falsehood grapple; who ever knew Truth put to the worse in free and open encounter?"

Notre Dame is privileged to be a part of this grand tradition of Catholic higher education. The search for truth, beauty, justice, and wisdom continues to require our best and most disciplined efforts. In pursuit of our high goal, freedom of inquiry has been our hallmark and our most effective resource. May it ever be thus.

The DuBois Lecture
on American Catholic
Higher Education

One of the great successes in the history
of the Catholic Church has been the establishment and the
prospering of Catholic private education—primary, secondary, and higher education—throughout the United States.

Against the grain of what was thought to be a hostile
culture with values alien to a Catholic view of reality, the
immigrant Church—largely from Europe—established first
a means of primary education for the young. This was done
not simply to prepare people for their lives, labors, and
professions but more to make them aware always—in the
workplace as well as at worship—what it meant to be a
Catholic Christian in this country.

Over time, as the aspirations of American Catholics grew,
this concept of education was extended to the secondary
level, and then gradually, to higher education. Recently
we celebrated the bicentennial of U.S. Catholic higher education with the anniversary of the founding of Georgetown University. Today, the list of Catholic colleges and
universities in this country numbers some 240, including my

own Notre Dame, where we are about to celebrate our 150th anniversary.

Having had the opportunity over the last several years to study Catholic higher education here and in other parts of the world, I have gained a new appreciation for the historic impact of our system. What it provided was a familiar and comfortable environment in which our immigrant generations and their successors could begin to realize their higher aspirations and achieve upward mobility in this land of opportunity.

The danger and threat were always that, as Catholics achieved a vested interest in American life, they would leave behind that core of their faith experience—identification with the Catholic community—and would consider themselves too sophisticated for what could begin to seem a naive or childlike faith. But because this educational network endured and grew stronger, because it successfully addressed the ongoing development of each new generation of students, it has been able to make a noteworthy contribution to the life of the Church as well as the life of the nation.

There are those, of course, both in this country and abroad, who still consider a Catholic college or university as a contradiction in terms. On the one hand, these people view Catholic institutions as inherently restrictive structures in which ideas are squelched, freedom is inhibited, and the full expansion and exploration of the world of the mind cannot take place. Because of the historical precedent of schools with former religious affiliations—beginning with Harvard and continuing on through much of private education—these people have accepted the notion that a full-fledged university cannot maintain a religious identity.

The secular educational tradition, then, has been associated with freedom, with achievement in the world of the mind, with beauty in the arts, and with the exploration of science and technology, while Catholic education has been seen as somehow cut off from these values.

But why should the concept of the Catholic university be a problem in the first place? In Rome recently a meeting of Catholic educators from around the world was held to discuss the nature of Catholic institutions and to try to advise the Holy Father and the bishops of the Church in the formulation of a document concerning Catholic higher education. During the course of these discussions, it became clear that a certain amount of suspicion existed, that some bishops had had experiences or been presented with claims suggesting that Catholic educational institutions were not being faithful to their identity or mission. On the other hand, Catholic educators felt beset by what they regarded as a small minority within the Catholic community who were continually barraging the leaders of the Church with complaints that amounted to nit-picking and ignored the full richness of Catholic higher education. Not surprisingly, then, as the debate unfolded, two basic positions emerged.

One maintained that a Catholic college or university is a branch of the institutional Church just as is a parish or a hospital or other institutions established by the Church. According to that point of view, any institution claiming to be Catholic must conform to a set of regulations or a body of instructions generated by the Church's institutional, hierarchical leadership.

The other position that emerged—the majority position in our conversations—regarded the university or college as first of all a particular human institution with its own history, traditions, structures, and operating procedures. According to this view of things, a university is Catholic not simply as a matter of origin, but rather because *as a university* it seeks to embody an explicitly stated set of values. This Catholic mission is its guide as it develops over time. At the same time, particularly in the Western tradition, the university maintains a life of its own, preserving its traditions of academic freedom; tenured professorships; structuring by departments, colleges or other academic units; entrusting student life to a particular administrative unit, academic life to another; and usually being governed by boards which are responsible for hiring and firing the university's administrators.

As the interplay developed between these two views— not necessarily contradictory, but also not easily melded— a strong consensus emerged and was reflected in the final formulations passed on to the Vatican congregation on education. These formulations—an attempt to state as explicitly as possible the essential elements of a Catholic college or university—are worthy of review.

The first element is mission or self-definition. Civil law, we know, recognizes a broad range of expressions of purpose and mission, which as long as they are consistently implemented cannot be overturned by law. A university or college can define itself, for example, as single sex, and by adhering consistently to that definition can avoid violating American constitutional law. Similarly, it can define itself as a religious institution either in general terms or by denomination.

A Catholic institution certainly ought to be explicit in its statement of its mission and aspirations. It ought to describe who within its structure exercises responsibility for the preservation of its Catholic identity, and, insofar as possible, it ought to describe its relationship with the institutional Church.

In America, most Catholic colleges and universities were established by religious communities of men and women or by diocesan clergy; the vast majority were not founded by Catholic Christian lay people. About twenty to twenty-five years ago, however, a major change took place in the organization of our institutions and in the assignment of responsibility for our institutional missions; in many cases this responsibility was given over to a predominantly lay board of control. These changeovers were acts of faith on the part of the religious communities or dioceses that formerly owned and controlled the institutions and also were acts of faith on the part of the Vatican congregations that approved the changeovers.

Today, at this particular stage in the development of Catholic higher education, it is even more important that these boards exercise full responsibility and that their authority be fully acknowledged.

The second element of Catholic identity concerns the faculty. To have a Catholic institution, it is important to have a core, a significant group of Catholic faculty who take their Catholic identity seriously. And in the very breath of saying that, I acknowledge the tremendous contribution and importance of faculty who are not Catholic but who bring their own conviction and experience into the common life and the common quest.

The nature of the academic hiring process makes it difficult even to ask about religious affiliation. There also is a resistance within academic units to give undue stress to religion compared with academic competence or areas of specialization that are particularly needed at a given time. Trying to strike the right balance between departmental and administrative priorities in the hiring of faculty has become one of the most critical processes that goes on in Catholic institutions.

The proportion of Catholic faculty members varies widely among Catholic colleges and universities. In many institutions, hiring in the humanities, particularly philosophy and theology, is thought to call for additional consideration of religious affiliation, and surely that is something that needs to be debated and discussed openly and fully by the board and the administration in interaction with the faculty. Obviously, if those most explicitly value-related disciplines are taught without sufficient concern for the mission and the identity of the university or college, that mission and identity will be apt to atrophy over time.

But there are other considerations that must be taken into account. One way that Catholic identity involves the faculty and curriculum is the way moral and ethical issues are addressed. For example, people who are being trained to practice in the business world: What issues ought one to expect to be taken up in the course of their education in a Catholic institution? What ethical dilemmas? What notions of responsibility, trustworthiness, and justice? If students are preparing to be engineers or architects, can they assume that the institution will attend not simply to questions of technical expertise but also to the much more difficult issues of ethical, responsible practice?

The same principle, of course, applies to research, to preparation as a physician or lawyer, to involvement in any of the professions. Not just Catholic faculty, but all faculty, whatever their discipline, need to acknowledge and agree that a Catholic institution should be a place where these kinds of conversations—concerning moral and ethical issue—will go on. Certainly there are faculty who are uncomfortable being asked to move outside their explicit training in graduate school, and yet when they do, they discover that the interaction is an enrichment for everyone involved—faculty instructing faculty, faculty learning from students, etc.

The third element of a Catholic college or university is the curriculum. Not only ought there to be a consistent ethical framework of reference in all courses and in the overall education provided, but also it is important to consider the interrelationships among disciplines.

Can we function without some kind of core curriculum? Without insisting on a hard and fast answer, surely there is precedent in Catholic institutions for maintaining that a liberal education has certain essential components. People who are the products of a liberal education ought to be reflective, knowledgeable about our background in the Western tradition, about how societies work, about our history as a species. They ought to have exercised their native curiosity about the world and all its parts. If that is not an essential part of what we are doing—if we are simply preparing people for immediate access to the workplace—then we are giving students short shrift.

The fourth element to be considered is the kind of research that ought to go on in Catholic institutions. One of the prime contributors to the prejudice that exists in much of academe—that a Catholic college or university is a contradiction in terms—is a belief that Catholic scholars are simply not interested in the world of high ideas, that they rush too quickly into practical applications of knowledge and that they are unwilling to take the risk of making mistakes or engaging in the critical process of high culture.

At the same time, there seems increasingly to be a desire —even among our secular college and university counterparts—for religiously affiliated schools to occupy a special leadership role concerning the great societal questions of the day, i.e., how do we analyze the options for responding to homelessness? Is there any quick fix? Is it simply a matter of charity, a kind of Mother Teresa approach, to take care of the people who are left in the streets at night? Surely that is one component of the response. Does it have to do with ascertaining whether the deinstitutionalization of the mentally ill was a mistake based on the presumption that neighborhood treatment centers would take up the slack (which didn't happen)? What has homelessness to do with the patterns of economic distribution in our society and can we change those patterns by alerting people to the injustice of the system?

Many of these questions cannot be considered as value judgments anywhere outside institutions such as ours. This is our moment of opportunity to take on some of the great issues of the day, to bring them into the classroom but also into our scholarly reflections, our research, and our writing. The shifting pressures among teaching and research and service are virtually a given in American higher education today. Some institutions give precedence to teaching, and treat research as fine in its place. Others stress research as a way to gain broader national recognition. Still others give a greater place to service, internally and externally. In a Catholic institution all three are important, but the way the balance is achieved will depend very much on the history and traditions of the particular school.

I will claim, however, that Catholic higher education has been most efficient not only in this country but around the world, in providing the kind of research and scholarship that can make a difference. The problem of homelessness is just one example. Extraordinary changes in geopolitics also are taking place. Radical turnovers of government have taken place in Eastern Europe and a continual pressure for democratization exists in the Soviet Union. The rough ending of at least direct Soviet government intervention in Afghanistan, the return of democratic government in Chile, and surprising elections in Nicaragua and other parts of the world all are part of a new tide of changes. An aspiration clearly exists in many parts of the world for a new order of things—an order that respects human life and human dignity. What institutions are better qualified than ours to lead the way in thinking through the implications for public policy of these very difficult and perplexing questions?

The fifth element of Catholic identity concerns how student life is organized and thought about in our institutions. A movement is afoot in American higher education to increase volunteer action on our campuses as an antidote to the "meism" and "looking out for number one" point of view that seems to have dominated the recent past. Most of us have personally discovered the value of volunteer action by being involved in service to the poor or the elderly or the young and by witnessing firsthand the poverty and injustice of life in Appalachia or the inner cities of our country, or the Third World. Exposing our students, staffs, and faculties to these realities will allow them to return to the interactions of the classroom with a new set of facts, new ideas, and a whole new agenda.

The time is right for looking at education in a holistic sense. What goes on in the classroom is crucial, and that work ought to be done as well and thoroughly as we can do it. The kind and quality of research produced by our faculties is significant. But it is also critical that all our campuses be touched by that momentum-building outreach that is student volunteerism today.

As an undergraduate I had the good fortune to become involved in a service project in Mexico, where I spent two months between my junior and senior years. Subsequently I spent two more summers in various parts of Latin America. I really believe that I have never been the same person since those experiences, and I thank God that so many people—on my campus and others around the country—have taken advantage of similar opportunities.

If this kind of compassion born in experience can be injected into the classroom, then we will begin to see truly thoughtful and reflective considerations of our options for the future, and this can literally transform the life of our campuses and the quality of interaction between faculty and students.

To cite a final element of identity, surely we are not Catholic universities or colleges unless we worship together. Prayer is at the heart of the Christian life. To recognize our fallibility, our weakness in the face of the temptation of academic arrogance, is crucial for us all individually and collectively. We need to have opportunities to step back from the fray for spiritual renewal and enlightenment, and we need extracurricular opportunities to build on our foundations in Christian life and practice.

All this is taken for granted in our self-definition. But unless we find a focus and point of integration for the many elements of our Catholicity, then I believe we will have failed to fulfill the great responsibility passed on to us out of the past.

I would say to faculty, can we find a way, develop a form of discourse, for struggling with this question of Catholic identity in an academically respectable way, recognizing the importance of the traditions of academic freedom, tolerance, debate, and dissent? Can we do that healthily, recognizing that it implies a certain degree of criticizing one another's work not only within the institution but across fields of expertise? Only when we can address the truth, acknowledge error, and discuss the difference between them will we really be doing our jobs in the world of the mind.

I say to administrators, we have been given a sacred trust. It is a tremendous balancing act when people on the left and on the right tend to be critical of the range of tolerant behavior and discourse that takes place on most of our campuses. We need to continue to assert our institutions' visions and the values that underlie them. We need to make hard decisions in hiring and in promotions and in institutional priorities. We need to raise money because it is crucial for institutional health and for preparing to meet the future. But we need to raise money not merely for its own sake but because we have a clear idea of how it can be put to good use.

We need, in short, to be both the consciences and the visionaries of our institutions.

I would say to students, please appreciate the intense concern shown you by the faculty and by those who work in student life, campus ministry, and in student residences. They care deeply about you, they really want you to develop as a whole person so that your life's decisions encompass not just what career paths you would like to follow or whether you would like to marry and whom, but also how to raise a family in a very complex world, the importance of worshipping in a community of faith, and the need to seek out opportunities to carry the value system you have learned here into the real life of your future.

The 240 Catholic colleges and universities of the United States constitute approximately half of the world's Catholic institutions of higher education. We have an opportunity not only to serve the people of this land, Catholic and non-Catholic alike, but also to be a model for the development of comparable institutions in others parts of the world. Perhaps the day of the hegemony of the European tradition in education is over. Much of the world looks to the United States for an illustration of what is possible in higher education; I would like to think the same is true for what is possible in Catholic higher education.

PART TWO

Challenges of Today's World

Discourse Between the Two Cultures: Science, Religion, and Humanities

*I*t is clear to me that many of us who live in multiple worlds sometimes suffer from a narrowness of vision. I am a priest and live as a Catholic Christian person who belongs to a particular religious denomination and tradition. I am also a teacher and a practitioner of the science of theology in the subspeciality of Christian ethics, and a university administrator. Yet I am sometimes embarrassed by those who claim to represent any of these worlds. It is possible for religious people to be very narrow-minded and unaware of what is going on around them and of the changes that are demanded by our culture and our time in history. It is possible for theologians to be so self-satisfied and convinced that they have risen above the human condition that they fail to take concrete human experience into account or to see their responsibility for the ramifications of their theoretical conclusions. In addition, it is possible for university administrators and all of those who would speak on behalf of the intellectual life to have such a restricted notion of the nature of a university that religion would have no place there. We would have such a parochial understanding of a university that it would cease to be a university in any real sense of the term.

I will begin by establishing some presuppositions, each of which would demand whole books to be covered adequately. I am simply going to assert them here, however, and give some indication of why I say what I do. In addition, I will make reference to some obstacles or problems in the relationship of science, religion, and the humanities. Then I will reflect upon some issues which allow us to see this sometimes precarious relationship through the discussion and rhetoric that come forth from the various institutions that represent science, religion and the humanities.

I believe that there is no such thing as a value-free science. There are all kinds of epistemological presuppositions built into that not very original claim. Max Weber—one of the founders of what we know as sociology—Thomas Kuhn, and others have reflected for our benefit upon the kind of relativity built into the questions that are asked and the answers that might be obtained from scientific research. We all would like to make some kind of claim for objectivity in our search for the truth. We would like, as much as we can, to free ourselves of bias, prejudice, and ideology in the sense of false consciousness. But in order to achieve that state, it seems to me, we would have to become so ethereal that we would resemble the angels about whom we speak in theological speculation. Human beings who practice the various sciences always bring their humanness to the endeavor. Part of what they bring are various kinds of value identifications and commitments, whether derived from the Enlightenment, or a specific religious tradition, or Marxist perspectives on reality, or from other sources. The so-called scientific method with its attempts to get at data so as to develop and test hypotheses, still is a function of the curiosity and inquisitiveness of human beings with particular intentions and points of view. The questions that we ask at least partially determine the answers that we are able to obtain.

As an ethicist, I have found interesting the burgeoning attention paid to biomedical ethics over the past quarter century. This has not occurred because everybody is innately interested in that area but because the money has been there, establishing think tanks like the Hastings Center in New York, the Kennedy Center at Georgetown University and many others. Had money been available elsewhere these scholars might have pursued other areas. The same thing is true more recently in business ethics. We have become focused on the economy today, at least with regard to ethical considerations, in a way that was not true two or three decades ago.

My second presupposition is that science is, or can be, a vocation. The language of vocation was employed by Martin Luther to describe what it meant to be a Christian in the world. From my vantage point, any search for the truth can be a route to God, whether it is for a given individual or for a community of scholars. Science can be a calling, a rich and fruitful way of trying to arrive at a greater approximation of the truth. If that is the case, I see it as something to which a person from my tradition might well be called to devote himself or herself.

My third presupposition is that the study of nature, including human nature, strives toward a unified theory. The academy today is too fragmented and stratified. In a sense we have become much like a physician who looks only at bones and not at the whole person. To a great extent, we are people who are interested in just one dimension of human experience. But it is only when we try to incorporate that knowledge and understanding into some broader view of nature, including human nature, that we can satisfy our curiosity about why things are the way they are and what it means to interact with the world.

Not only does the academy today disregard the desirability of a unified theory of knowledge, it disavows the consequences of its findings. So what if my theory leads to certain results? So what if we can make some kind of connection between Hegel and Hitler? So what if somebody's theory about the worth of a certain segment of the human family leads us to practices which demean civilization? It seems to me that built into the particular study of some phenomenon, including the human phenomenon or any part of it, is the demand that we try to see the connection between that specific piece of knowledge and the way we perceive and understand all reality.

A fourth presupposition is that reason counts. Arguments do count. The weakest form of argument, even though a legitimate form, is the appeal to authority. I believe that one of the richest parts of the particular philosophical and theological tradition that is my own—a broad Western tradition which is specifically Roman Catholic—is a respect for reason. It is not the case that our hearts, our experiences, and our feelings do not speak to us as well; it is a confidence that, given sufficient time and effort and goodwill, people can arrive at a working and effective consensus about matters of public dispute and disagreement. Only if we trust in that process, only if we believe that words and symbols can allow us to get at the truth and to communicate effectively, can we have some kind of handle that will allow us to make progress toward mutual understanding. One of the things that I most fear in our time—perhaps it has always been present—is that people will simply categorize those who disagree as irrational or oblivious to the truth, that they will cease to try to communicate and will cease to arrive at some kind of consensus about troubling issues, especially in the public forum.

Finally, I believe as an ethicist that one of the most difficult and perplexing things about the relationship of science and religion and the humanities is how to move from value language to normative, principled, rule-oriented language. How do we go from the most general claims about where our hearts are, symbolically or metaphorically, from where we stand as unique human beings with values that attract us or give a power and a beauty and a kind of resonant spirit to our lives, to the more difficult description of normative kinds of claims which require precision of language? How do we take the step to a principled language and do we think principles will enable us to make universal claims or are they just roughly useful? When it comes to public policy matters, most of us would like to be able to move at least to the level of principle, because if we can show the transition from values which may be widely held to principles, we can make at least some progress on matters of public conversation.

What are the problems we can identify as we try to find some bridges across the bounds of science, religion, and the humanities? From the vantage point of the religiously committed person, the first problem is what might be called the "scientific imperative." Is it true to say that whatever we can do by way of research or exploration, we ought to do? Beyond that, should we fund such projects if we have an opportunity to commit our resources for that purpose? The federal government and major institutions, including the business community, are responsible for subsidizing most of the research that goes on in the American academy. There are choices to be made about where we should put our resources. It seems to me that the bald claim that there is such a thing as the "scientific imperative" and that all research that can be done ought to be done is misguided. I think we must make a connection between our value judgments, i.e., the knowledge we believe should have the highest priority, and how we allocate our limited resources.

I believe that one of the most important hallmarks of any profession is a code of conduct, and this ought to apply to the scientific community in both the natural and the social sciences. I reject the view that the scientific imperative ought to reign supreme. I think scientific research and the support for it ought to be determined on the basis of values and that hard choices ought to be made along the way.

A second problem has to do more with religion than science. Religious tradition is inherently conservative because it seeks to preserve the memories of certain great events of the past and to reinterpret ancient traditions for the contemporary world. In this there always will be a certain suspicion about the new, the radical, the "breakthrough."

We can recall extreme instances in Western history: the Inquisition, the rack, the ordeal, all instituted supposedly to obtain the truth, and largely with the approval of theologians and religious leaders. However seriously misguided, for a time these terrors were considered appropriate responses to the new, the challenging, and the revolutionary. We see the same process at work in religious responses to the ideas of Galileo, Darwin, Marx, Freud, and others. In fact, virtually every revolutionary thinker was held suspect by the religious leaders of the day. One of the challenges, then, for the intellectual representatives of religious traditions, including Christianity, is to find an effective way to mediate new knowledge and to demonstrate that it is not necessarily incompatible with tradition. As we recognize in looking at some such issues, this is not always easy to accomplish.

A related problem is fundamentalism. What I mean by fundamentalism is a belief that control of the sacred text is control of the thought processes of the adherents. It is an attempt to disallow any recognition of the evolution of thought or the importance of what is called "hermeneutics," the science of interpretation.

Because people sometimes feel threatened and picture the world in dire, apocalyptic terms, fundamentalism can take on an authoritarian form that extends its influence from the church in the broader society. Humans always look to the future for fulfillment in this world, and one of the tasks of religion is to interpret the world as something other than the be-all and end-all of existence. Fundamentalism addresses a very basic human need for stability, order, and assurance, yet it errs because it claims to assure or guarantee access to the truth by controlling the text or controlling the process of communication within a religious tradition or imposing its view on the civil order.

The tensions among science, religion, and the humanities are well illustrated by a number of contemporary issues. The first is criminal behavior. We know from the history of criminology that there have been various attempts by scientists to explain why people act the way they do. One theory at a particular moment of history was that our forehead shape could determine whether we had criminal tendencies. This science of phrenology was taken quite seriously. In old criminology texts one sees heads in side and front views, with blacked out eyes, especially gigantic foreheads found among criminals in prison—the results, of course, of very selective sampling.

Another attempt to define criminality was body shape, and more recently we have had the xyy, or "super male chromosome" claim that certain kinds of genetic testing could identify those with a propensity to become sociopaths. In short, we have a tradition of attempts by science to try to account for why we do evil. From the vantage point of religion, however, the concepts of original sin and temptation appear every bit as credible as notions of head or body size or shape.

Is it nature or nurture that leads us to perform evil deeds against one another? Are criminals simply sick? Are criminals so environmentally determined that they have no freedom left to control their behavior? Or is it a fact that people can be held morally accountable for their deeds? It seems to me that there are partial explanations available on the basis of scientific evidence, but I have seen no persuasive or even plausible explanation for criminal behavior that does not take into account human freedom and the context within which human freedom is properly exercised.

We have a great debate in our culture centering on various concepts including deterrence, retribution, rehabilitation, and isolation. At one time, the rationale of our criminal justice system was that we could rehabilitate criminals by putting them in jail, but no evidence conclusively shows this. Incarceration might possibly deter; it is hard to prove. One might believe in retribution or righting the wrong; one might think we can rehabilitate, but only under highly controlled conditions. But one thing we surely can do is isolate. Should we, then, only put in prison people who we think need to be isolated? We face a great crisis over the prospect of building more prisons and incarcerating an ever-growing percentage of the population. How we explain criminal behavior will inevitably shape our views on the handling of criminals.

A second question is alcoholism. Why are some people alcoholics and other people not? Is alcoholism a disease? There seems good reason to believe that it is and that we should treat its sufferers with all the respect that goes along with that acknowledgment. Yet alcoholism seems also to be a function of social conditioning. People who live in a society where nobody drinks are liable never to discover that they are or could be alcoholics. The availability of alcohol opens up the possibility for somebody who is predisposed, like the Irish or American Indians, to become alcoholic. I do not know of any extended Irish family—including my own—that does not have at least one alcoholic member. The availability of alcohol and the social structures that support heavy drinking increase the possibility that alcoholism might become a problem for a given individual.

What about moral blame? We have a very curious phenomenon in that the most successful therapy available for alcoholism is provided by Alcoholics Anonymous. Alcoholics Anonymous claims to be a nondenominational, nonreligiously affiliated group, but in its twelve steps one must appeal to a higher power, some source outside of one's self to whom one is accountable. One makes amends by going to all the people that one has harmed along the way and asking for their forgiveness. Each member tries to be open and confessional; that is interesting, isn't it? One is confessional in front of the group in saying "I am an alcoholic."

Science has forced religion to take into account a dimension of the experience of alcohol abuse that religion on its own grounds might never have had to do. We now find a boundary point where we have redescribed, even on religious grounds, alcoholism as a disease, but we have simultaneously tried to preserve the notion of moral accountability.

Organ transplantation is another issue with moral implications. I am on the Indiana Governor's Commission on Organ Donation and we make recommendations for public policy with regard to many sensitive normative issues. The questions we face include determining the criteria for patient selection. How are we going to foster the giving of organs? Should we take them? Should we presume consent unless the opposite is proven? Or should we have a process for giving consent for organ donation? At one time that was a very controversial issue. Most people I know agree that organ donation is a good thing, but there are questions over how we do it and who gets access to it. Should the president go on television to argue the case for a particular recipient— some little girl somewhere–when there are fifty or a hundred or a thousand other people who have equal claim to the same organ or to comparable organs? Organ donation is one example where religious belief and altruistic motivations are very much related to the amelioration of a significant social, biomedical problem.

We live in a pluralistic culture. Therefore, public debate on the matters I have mentioned is crucial. The work of the Miller Center and of other similar institutions to help people become informed and recognize the connection between the values that they have (whether religiously inspired or not) and the kind of civil responsibilities that they bear is particularly important at this moment in our history. Otherwise, the decisions may be made by the few so-called experts or may be made by default by those less qualified than ourselves to exercise our options.

In addition, we need to try to persuade rather than to coerce. Yet the temptation of the elite in religion, in intellectual life, and in the body politic is always to act on behalf of everybody else. We say on the one hand that we trust the common lot of humanity, that this is a democracy and republican form of government and that popular rule is deeply rooted in our traditions, and yet we all think that "the masses are asses and the elite are effete." We suspect elitism, and yet we really do not have a great confidence in the mass of humanity. We struggle from the desire to be coercive, especially if we are gifted with words or with knowledge of the political process. We want to skip the steps that are necessary for people to know what they are doing and to give common assent to it.

Finally, we will continue to live in an interdependent world. Whether a scientist or a humanist is also a religious adherent or not, he or she must take into account the rights of religious people to have a say in the decisions of the government, in university life, and in the priorities that we establish for ourselves. I believe a university is the most fruitful place to promote this kind of interaction. I only hope that Notre Dame and all the other great universities and colleges of this country can serve not only the scientific community but also the Church to keep us all honest and to keep us all in conversation.

Question: I believe you used the term the "science of theology." Were you speaking in an empirical sense or in a disciplinary sense?

Father Malloy: In a disciplinary sense. I think theology is a science, a legitimate science, in the sense that it has its own procedures, accepted methods of exploration, standards of argumentation, and historical tradition with which one can become familiar, for example, in doctoral studies. Then there are journals; there are recognized outstanding theologians whom one can study; and there are some people who wield a greater influence by virtue of their expertise at a particular moment. One needs to display sufficient acquaintance with that tradition and the ability to employ its language and methodology in order to win acceptance as a qualified practitioner. I do not mean theology is simply an empirical study, but rather, theology is a recognized discipline, comparable in its own way to chemistry or history or law.

Question: What do you think of the importance of teaching creationism in schools and of the recent court ruling in Alabama on secular humanism?

Father Malloy: I do not think the recent ruling in Alabama will stand the test of the Appeals Court, so the decision in itself is not going to last in terms of the judicial process. Creationism is an interesting thing, but as a Catholic, I feel a certain distance from it. There was a time in Catholic theology when a creationist-evolution controversy might have arisen, but the main stream of Catholic thought moved away from that point and has absorbed modern biblical criticism. Once that is done—even if it requires some decisions about how far to push the methodology—there is room for an interpretation of the text that acknowledges the problem of evolution. In other words, there is nothing incompatible between certain basic notions of evolution and elements of the Christian belief system such as the stories in the Book of Genesis or various parts of the Old Testament.

I do think, however, that those who object to certain notions of evolution (such as either Darwinian survival of the fittest or a kind of embedded, Enlightenment, anti-theistic position) have a good point. It is also possible, for example, that somebody could do a history of America and not take into account the history of religion or the role of the churches in America. It seems to me that this is very poor history because it does not recognize how the churches have, in many ways, been the most important element in influencing the value system of the people of this country. The notions of the Bible Belt, the preachers out on horseback, and the tent meetings represent how democratized religion has become in the American experience.

I would say that it is possible to give a fair accounting of evolution in any textbook. It is a theoretical position which seems to account for a lot of phenomena in a way that nothing else does. One can push it too far, however, as an utter or a complete explanation which would be exaggerated or inappropriate. So I think the critics are forcing certain elements of the scientific community to be more humble and limited in the way they present scientific theory. Nonetheless the evolutionists can say to the creationists, "You cannot give as full an explanation of the world as we can and until you can, you should not represent yourself as equal and adequate scientific theorists."

Question: I would like you to address the problem of society that finds nearly everybody educated in only one of three streams of thought: religious, scientific, or humanistic. They do not speak on the same terms with one another, thus limiting their interaction. How do you deal with the problem of those three groups communicating with each other since they each have a kind of distinct personality?

Father Malloy: The easiest answer is for the same person to be in all three groups. Is it possible for a scientist to be a believer? Some could imagine that it is not, yet I know people whom I consider excellent scientists who are believers and are also very well educated so as to be open to the arts and to the broader notion of human well-being. When this breadth is not in the same person, then human mechanisms like friendship, working on common projects, looking for areas of consensus, and minimizing areas of conflict have to suffice. As with any groups which start out on different wavelengths, there are problems. What I fear most is the case of individuals who represent different strata of society sitting back and hurling diatribes at one another. As a result they do not increase the communication at all, but rather increase the level of suspicion and antagonism and elicit from the other side something comparable. That is not my style and it is not at all productive in the long run.

Let me give an example of a productive way to overcome these problems. There is a man who graduated from Notre Dame named Jim Muller who teaches at the Harvard Medical School. He was one of the cofounders of Physicians for Nuclear Responsibility which won the Nobel Peace Prize. He learned Russian when he was at Notre Dame and he became concerned about the whole question of nuclear deterrence and the possibility of nuclear holocaust. When he went to Russia on some research projects he was able to speak the language of the people. When the possibility came along of trying to bring Russian and American scientists together, he had a headstart because he had already established a rapport with people on medical grounds. That led to the broader concern about the survival of our two cultures, which for him was linked to his religious convictions as a Catholic. It so happened that when he went to the Nobel Peace Prize ceremony, a Russian physician there had a heart attack on the stage. He came up to the stage where some people were working on the physician—many were cardiologists—and the medical people from Sweden examined him and said, "He's dead; it is too late for him." But Jim said, "No, I think there is still a chance to save him." Jim stuck with him and worked on him until they got to the hospital, and the physician lived. So in the very ceremony at which they all received the Nobel Prize together, he saved the life of a Russian physician who subsequently was very instrumental in gaining greater cooperation in the project from the Soviet government. That is an example that nobody could have predicted, of how getting involved in one project can lead to a higher level of communication and mutual trust. It then led to the possibility of getting other people involved in the same kind of conversation.

Beyond that, I do not have any magic scheme. Father Hesburgh has as his number one priority to work from within Notre Dame's Institute for International Peace Studies to bring people together. He has focused on scientists first of all because he believes that the scientists are most in touch with the potential for ill that goes along with the use of nuclear weapons, and because of that they can have an influence on their cultures that nobody else can have. Therefore, we brought together at Notre Dame a group of retired Soviet generals and a group of retired American generals to talk for a period of time about their experience of war and what they think of the nuclear question. We brought three people from the U.S.S.R., three from China, three from the United States, and one each from Japan, France, England and Germany, all under twenty-five years of age, to spend a year earning Masters degrees in Peace Studies together, to try to prepare the next generation of leaders to know each other, to speak the same language and to have some common concerns on which they can cooperate. I think what we are doing is great. It is the kind of thing that can work better than simply sitting back and thinking that the scientists are all merely absorbed in their own work and have no sense of humanity or that the humanists are out of it or that the religious people are Neanderthals.

Question: What are your views on research in the area of *in vitro* fertilization?

Father Malloy: The main objections to *in vitro* fertilization that appeared early on in the literature were classic ones. Is it a threat to the notions that we have presumed about sexuality and the relationship between genital intercourse and the bearing of children? Is there something very unique about blood bonding and the way that one identifies with a child as wholly one's own? I think these are legitimate questions.

A second concern has to do with what has been called "playing God." Are we presuming a kind of wisdom that can only be tested by time? Will we discover after the fact that we regret having promoted this kind of step?

A third concern revolves around the rejection of some of the fertilized eggs, that we could see as an abortive process. If you believe, as I do, that you have human life from the moment of fertilization and therefore, a protectable human life—all things being equal—and you deliberately reject some of the fertilized eggs, then this is a serious concern.

An objection which I do not find very persuasive has to do with the way that the sperm is obtained for *in vitro* fertilization.

In the end, the real debate is whether this is an excessive mechanization of a natural process under the guise of doing good for infertile couples. Will the results in the end destroy the delicate fabric of the family concept and parental bonding as we have known it throughout human history? I do not think the answers are yet available to these questions. I think one needs to be wary and at least concerned about the significance of *in vitro* fertilization, even if restricted to a couple. Still, I think that one can look at the arguments for and against it and can at least entertain the possibility that it can be a moral procedure.

Once it extends beyond the marital bond, then I think we have a different situation, one that I would find morally objectionable because of what it does to the notion of family. It is possible now to have five parents: the donor of the egg and the sperm, a host mother, and the nurturing couple. It is possible in the same way to have lesbian parents, homosexual male parents, single parents, elderly parents or juvenile parents. You could reconstruct the whole understanding of parenting on this basis, which brings to mind the notion of human hatcheries from the *Brave New World*. All of this is good reason, if not for alarm, then at least for deep and consistent concern.

Question: There is a great new debate about papal teachings. As an ethicist and an academician, what is your view on that question? Does papal proclamation completely and finally end debate and what is your view on the Church's quick, decisive reaction when dissent has been repeatedly vocal?

Father Malloy: Well, it is hard to know where to begin on that question. In studying church history, whether Catholic, Protestant or any other, there are certain periods that are more marked by conflict than others. Certain issues rise to prominence and become a kind of test of orthodoxy. It is lamentable from my point of view that so much of the discussion about authentic teaching and orthodoxy has revolved around sexual morality. It seems to me that there is a wide sweep of concerns (of which sexuality is only one) which we might employ to see where somebody is within the broader context of the Catholic community or any other community.

For instance, Michael Novak, William Simon, William O'Brien, and others came out with a letter about the nuclear question in which they pushed the matter of the criteria of just war past its traditional interpretations. William O'Brien said in his response to the Bishop's letter on war and peace—this is from a conservative perspective—that the principle of noncombatant immunity or discrimination was not an overarching moral principle that should buttress any judgment about war. Rather, it was a beginning point or a *prima facie* duty, and that the evil of the Soviet system with its threat to all the freedoms that we know was sufficient to override the immorality of deterrence as a nuclear strategy. Hence we should be prepared to fight a limited nuclear war. He argued the case that we should start by limited targeting but be prepared, if necessary, to implement targeting for total devastation.

That goes against the grain of all that I know in just war thought as it evolved out of the Catholic tradition. O'Brien, then, is a dissenter. Michael Novak argues the case for an extension of the notion of right intention, which is way beyond what I think has been true in much of the discussion in the Catholic community and even in the broader Christian community about right intention as a criterion of just war. Novak, then, is a dissenter.

I do not say that they should not be able to voice their dissent because that depends on what issue, on where dissent lies, and on how much freedom of discussion people wish to tolerate. I am on the progressive end of the spectrum when it comes to the range of the exploration of ideas and allowance for disagreement, especially in a university setting. I think the university is the proper context within which to do it.

However, individuals should acknowledge that they, are at odds with the inherited traditional position. I think that acknowledgment needs to be part of good teaching and good writing. Yet in the Catholic intellectual world today, the great hope is in this country where we have more qualified and committed scholars than in any other part of the world. The European tradition is much more suspicious of what goes on here than it ought to be, especially considering the quality of life and worship of the Catholic community in general. I wish Europeans could spend more time here and learn firsthand the kinds of things that are going on and see the wide range of issues that are being taken up. They should see what the American political tradition has done to the notions that Catholics have and what ought to happen in the life of the church. I think the university community needs to try to preserve the discourse as much as possible. That does not mean that we should be centers of some kind of hostile opposition although there are always going to be celebrated cases of individual opposition.

At my institution, the most conservative Catholics, fairly liberal Catholics, and all the range in between are represented. We have very few really radical types on our faculty. I like the diversity; I think it is healthier than just being identifiable as one kind of Catholic university. Whether or not Rome will like that is not for me to say. It is for me to try to represent it well and to build bridges, rather than try to breed conflict.

Ethics In the Workplace

*E*very Christian person is under a biblical mandate to make manifest in his or her concrete situation the operative moral values of love, justice, mercy, respect for God and his creation. We live in a time in history when the Church has largely abandoned the too easy separation of the world into sacred and secular spheres. Unlike Martin Luther whose Two Kingdoms theory suggested that, of necessity, different standards prevailed in the domestic sphere from those in the public order, contemporary Roman Catholic thought has increasingly urged that the task of the community of faith is to transform the world.

Above all, we are to be sacraments or signs of God's presence in the world. Despite the inevitable temptation to cynicism and despair, we are to promote, by both our informed discourse and our compassionate example, a mode of trusting and collaborative response to the perceived human needs of our time. We are to respond to perplexing problems such as how to distribute goods equitably, how to provide decent housing and sufficient work, how to calm racial and ethnic antagonisms, how to ensure responsible government. Our overarching desire is that the power of God's kingdom be made effective even now. It is a conviction which can be sustained in hope despite all the resistance we might encounter. Only such a transcendent claim can shake us loose from our complacency and inertia. If we would be activists with a real capability for enthusiasm and persistence, we must continually recognize that the source of our confidence is a God who has not abandoned us to our own schemes and devices but rather has gifted us with the power of his Spirit.

The first point, therefore, is that there is no world apart, no isolated enclave, where a Christian perspective on reality does not apply. You are the same person when you lead public worship or confront an unproductive employee, console the recently widowed or grapple with government regulations. The same basic commitments are at stake. There is no place but this fragile, sin-filled world where you can manifest that the Lord of history has taken over your life and charged you with responsibility, a responsibility for developing clarity of vision and sensitivity of judgment vis-à-vis the social, economic, and political environment within which we all live.

Most, if not all of you, pursue an occupation within the framework of social market capitalism, the prevailing American economic model. Social market capitalism is a historical modification of the earlier laissez-faire capitalism and an alternative to the major ideological options of Marxism and democratic socialism. I mention this here not to pursue an extensive discussion of these various systems, but rather to alert us to the fact that one level of analysis about Christian decision making related to work has to do with an affirmation or rejection of these major theories as compatible or not with the Christian Gospel.

I would summarize the current state of discussion on this question by pointing to the papal social encyclical tradition which has been equally critical of each of the alternatives whenever and insofar as they neglected the dignity of the individual worker, promoted violent class conflict, refused to allow subsidiary levels of responsibility, or promised a materialistic paradise. It seems that there is no Christian economic system as such, but rather a series of more or less adequate options, no one of which is probably suitable for the great range of social and political circumstances that exist throughout the world.

For those who may favor an economic system other than social market capitalism, the following reflections may seem otiose or superficial. I am not so much interested in arguing the case for the superiority of our particular economic configuration as I am in presuming its pervasiveness. As much as we might regret the various inequities perpetrated by the existing system (legitimated unemployment, sharp disparities in opportunity, a ruthless competitiveness), our desire to be effective moral agents must come to grips with this *given* in our cultural matrix.

Hard cases make for interesting classes but overdrawn ethical theories. While I am not adverse to the use of challenging examples as an opportunity for insight into how theory and practice come together, I think it is a disservice to Christian moral reflection to overlook the ordinary and typical as the prime source for our sense of things. In this spirit, I will highlight what I take to be some recurrent dilemmas for the Christian worker in America.

One of the burdens of our media-oriented existence is that we are bombarded with an endless stream of poorly digested information, conjecture, and opinion. Conflicting accounts of the same phenomenon (a traffic accident, an illness, urban decay) prompt us to doubt that we will ever be certain of the truth.

And yet our very lives as Christians are based upon the claim that Jesus came as the Word of God, the revealer of the ultimate truth about the human condition and the human prospect. Respect for the truth has been a revered virtue throughout Christian history. To deliberately deceive, to lie without extenuating circumstances, has been pictured as a classic form of evil-doing. But it may be that the more threatening form of violation of our collective right to the truth is a sustained and calculated silence in the face of a reality that needs to be exposed.

For example, in the relationship between nearly every set of employers and employees there is a thin veil of mutual consent drawn over the personal idiosyncrasies of those involved. It is a kind of subtle blackmail in which the only things that can be criticized are objective factors like: level of productivity, tardiness, or insubordination. What is left unsaid are all the obvious self-deceptions and instances of social ineptness which create jealousy, resentment, and pettiness. The dynamic of relationships cannot be reduced, machine-like, to external criteria but must encompass those difficult to discern patterns of aggrandizement and abuse.

However, the temptation to calculated silence exists not only in the interaction in a particular work situation but also in its relationship to the individuals or groups it serves. Like Western pioneers gathered in a circle for self-protection, collaborators in work can assume a defensive posture which justifies all kinds of chicanery—the sale of inferior products, half-hearted research, nepotism, protection of the incompetent and the addicted. The immediate fear in speaking out is that one will be fired or at best rendered suspect in the eyes of one's colleagues. Whistle-blowers are quickly isolated lest their excessive candor contaminate the rest of the participants in a common enterprise. In such circumstances, silence and feigned tolerance are an easier solution than a potentially explosive public revelation of the truth.

What I am suggesting by way of these two examples is that one kind of recurring problem for Christian workers and employers is how to maintain a concern for, and commitment to, the truth in the face of various pressures, both self-induced and socially reinforced. Patterns of initiation into the work situation often confuse the issue by so stressing the importance of loyalty to the company or union that a concern for truth-telling is seen as a vestigial remnant of a naive world view. If this dilemma rings true to your own experience, then further reflection on the Christian value of truthtelling is called for.

In a growth economy full of unlimited promise, it requires little justice to give everyone their share. But in the midst of

a haunting recession, high unemployment, and major industrial relocation, the cutting edge of respect for human dignity
is preserved at a price. The divisions among groups become
sharper and there rises a creeping recognition that there
may not be enough to go around. Families go on the road
as they pursue rumor suggesting the availability of stable
work. Cities become gathering places of the marginal and the
poor. International competition closes factories and breeds
a mentality favorable to corporate takeovers. Obviously, in
terms of all of this, it is easy to forsake principles readily
adhered to in better times.

One way to formulate the challenge is to suggest that
fair treatment—a demand of justice based on the inherent
worth of each human agent—can give way to a generalized
disrespect for whole categories of people described solely
in terms of their disfunctional traits. Thus, for example, our
society faces in inconsistent fashion the problem of retire-
ment. We live longer than any other people in history and
therefore are potentially a part of the work force for much
of that span. Yet the drive toward upward mobility for the
young leads to resentment toward the older age groups and
a consequent temptation to concoct explanations for why
their presence as workers is counterproductive. Impossible
assignments, unsettling time schedules, decreased responsibility, contract buy-outs can all be means of ridding ourselves
of the unpleasant reality of aging. On the other hand, a
social group or economic unit that does not make room for
the infusion of youthful energy and new ideas will soon be
outstripped by its rivals. The standard of fair treatment would
seem to require that individuals be judged, not in terms of
some pejorative categorization that discounts their particular
personal qualities and history of contribution, but rather by
humane criteria that acknowledge the diversity of roles that
different age groups can play in the same collective effort.

A second dilemma of this kind is related to the broad
debate over affirmative action, equal access, and minority
quotas. In the crassest terms, this political struggle can be
seen as a power move by select groups to gain a greater

percentage of a diminishing pie. However, in a more positive light, it is a belated attempt to right the injustices of a national history in which slavery, prejudice, and discrimination have skewed the opportunity for equality in housing, education, and the job market.

An integral part of the disagreement about a national policy to provide fair treatment for minority groups, women, and the physically or mentally impaired is how to deal with the period of transition. For a variety of reasons some individuals from these broad categories will not be properly prepared or sufficiently confident to succeed in the new work situations. It becomes imperative then to help employers and employees from the more traditional workforce to make proper judgments about the differences between individuals and categories of individuals. Employers especially have an obligation to reexamine their attitudes and practices to ascertain whether they are treating individuals simply as instances of categories in making decisions about hiring and retention.

Unless there are sufficient jobs for all available workers, which is unlikely in the present situation, the choice of one person is the rejection of another. For example, the influx of women into previously all-male settings requires not only adjustments of patterns of interaction, but also a concern for related matters such as pregnancy leaves and child care. To be an advocate of equal opportunity for women without being willing to finance the necessary support structures is to consign fair treatment to the unrealizable domain of sheer speculation.

A third case in which fair treatment is difficult to achieve is in connecting promotion and career advancement to a nomad-like succession of moves. For the single person, this scenario may add some excitement and motivation to their present work responsibility. But to the married employee there are severe hardships that can come from interrupting the schooling of the children and trying to sell or rent a house in a poor real estate market. Sometimes one party commutes long distances on the weekend just to preserve some semblance of domestic life. All of this is doubly complicated when both spouses work, as they often do now, and one is being pressured by the other to leave behind an enjoyable career. Large corporations, the entertainment industry, the military, and government service all presuppose that the married person should be willing to accommodate his or her family life to the changing priorities and personnel distribution of the employing agency.

What these three illustrations should convey is that fair treatment in the workplace is complicated by the human tendency to categorize whole groups of individuals as unworthy of respect because they fail to satisfy certain criteria of usefulness. They may be characterized as dull and enfeebled through age, or improperly trained, or too demanding of job-related benefits, or unwilling to allow their lives to be dominated by work. Whatever the excuse that rationalizes our conduct, our perplexing task is to sort out the relevant factors and to reduce the limitations we subjectively impose so that justice will fully be served.

The power of positive thinking and looking out for Number One dovetail nicely in the picture of the respectable, successful, and independent seeker of economic good fortune and control over his or her material destiny. The myths of American life play down the covetous instinct as necessarily harmful and instead seek to redescribe it as the source of creativity and initiative-taking. Even the dynamic of supply and demand can be seen as a stimulus to beneficial coalitions and the encouragement of cooperative behavior. Instead of a war of all against all, the economic forum becomes an arena for the best manifestations of discipline and personal control in the guise of the hard-driving entrepreneur and the effective technician.

Within this widely propagandized view of reality, integrity is nothing more than an individual's conformity to his or her privately validated value system. Despite the general cheerfulness of its proponents (they can often make a living giving motivational pep talks to business conferences), such a vision reduces the self to an unanchored existence in which the other is, at first view, more a rival than a friend. Expectations of trust and confidence are relegated to the home or to small circles of companions.

The Christian picture of the desired shape of things is much different. We hope for mutual enlightenment and a shared vision. Drawing upon the stories of our collective past, we probe them for insight and reassurance. Because we depend upon God for all that is worthwhile in our lives, we have the courage to acknowledge our interdependence. For us, integrity is a shared challenge as we both rebuke and console one another. In the final judgment, our integrity or moral disgrace are revealed by both the major decisions which shape the contours of our daily existence and by the consistency and intensity with which we pursue the good.

A striking example of the centrality of this virtue of personal integrity is our response to the question: Is there any manner of earning a living that a Christian in conscience could not undertake? We might think instinctively of the professional killer, the torturer, or the prostitute. Yet that would be too easy. Are there not other positions in our society that a morally sensitive Christian person would have to refuse?

What would we say about the politician functioning in a governmental structure suffused with corruption and graft? Would tolerance of pervasive abuse of the public trust be tantamount to an assent to the acceptability of such patterns? Even if the individual remained personally aloof, could he or she maintain a sense of dignity in the midst of such wholesale corruption?

Commentators on the contemporary scene have looked closely and found a host of situations of similar import. In a world horrifyingly on the brink of thermonuclear war, missiles are being constructed and submarines being directed by Christians who must ponder seriously their role in the potential holocaust. In medical facilities, scientific research and its resulting technology have brought to the fore issues related to fertilization and birth, artificial sustenance and death, that are sources of discomfort to those who must sometimes implement the choices of others with which they morally disagree.

At whatever level our participation might occur, we must wonder whether there is ever good reason for a definitive "no." Should there not be a Rogue's Gallery in the Christian Church of those representative positions in the labor force which have so much villainy attached that they are to be renounced at whatever personal hardship—the drug runner, those who prey on the elderly and young, the professional gossip, the fomenter of violence?

Insofar as we can imagine such a possible range of forms of work to be rejected, we can perhaps more clearly recognize the challenges to personal integrity that arise from the concrete circumstances of our lives.

There are a number of dimensions of our economic system which individuals of moral sensitivity have an added responsibility to be aware of. We cannot help but notice the ways in which the economic values of our society influence our behavior and our cultural mores. A brief catalogue of several such items will help to make the point.

We Americans are consumers in unprecedented ways. It seems as though our appetites for food, clothing, trinkets, conveniences, vehicles, etc. are unlimited. Compared to some hypothetical person or family portrayed in seductive advertising, we may seem deprived. Yet we know, deep in our hearts, that we could get by with much less. We overindulge and then spend a fortune on diet books and health care. We merchandise in open rooms, begging the shopper to reach out, and wonder why shoplifting and theft are rampant.

On the other hand, there is a perpetual attraction to simplicity. We fondly recall the era of our ancestors who often struggled just to survive and to put bread on the table. And further back we hear the haunting words of Jesus about the danger of riches and the special favor God shows to the poor and forsaken.

How else but by reflecting critically on the creeping dangers of affluence can we avoid its contagion? And at what point will an agenda for collective action emerge? The professing Christian should surely be in the forefront of such an effort.

In some parts of contemporary church life there is sustained attention given to structured questions of economic injustice. In light of this analysis, a number of strategies have been developed for effecting positive change. Presuming that the description of the situation is accurate, there can still be legitimate disagreement about the proposed remedies. For example, because the American Catholic Church under the leadership of Cardinal Gibbons supported the labor movement in the second half of the nineteenth century, there is a strong undercurrent of pro-union sentiment in the Catholic heritage. Many important goals of social justice— fair wages, safe working conditions, sick leave, pensions— have been implemented under the auspices of the unions. Yet we find that a decreasing percentage of American workers belong to unions and that the bureaucratization of the movement has sometimes led to corruption and the protection of entrenched interests. International competition in the labor market has called into question the feasibility of meeting increased union demands without a corresponding improvement in worker productivity.

Unions seem to be one vehicle among several possibilities for protecting the rights of the working class. We need to be able to talk sensibly about the economic situations which maximize their usefulness. The same is true for boycotts, shareholder actions, and other means for holding the system accountable to its own high promises.

The influx of refugees from Southeast Asia, Haiti, Poland, and Central America, as well as the long-range issue of migration from Mexico, has reminded us that hospitality is hardest when the guests stay on. Surely there are some occupations that have almost no appeal to even the impoverished American. But these jobs can absorb only a limited percentage of the immigrant population. What do we do with the rest?

Not only are language and cultural barriers sources of local tension, but the impression that refugees replace native workers and exacerbate the unemployment problem is enough to revive the nativist sentiments of the past. We desperately need a reasonable national policy on immigration. We need to purge the laws of racist presuppositions at the same time that we acknowledge that our capability for absorbing large numbers is presently being tested.

There is much debate today about economy of scale in corporate life. It seems as though, at the level of the multinational, the government of a specific nation loses control over the policies and practices that characterize its corporate actors. On the other hand, this cross-cultural capability can enable multinationals to mobilize available resources more effectively. In our delicate, interdependent world economy there is a need for long-range planning and crisis management. The outbreak of war in the Middle East can temporarily cripple the industrial nations of the West. The hegemony of Japan in automobiles and electronics can eliminate jobs across the U.S. One response to this threat to national economic sovereignty is to reestablish protectionist statutes. "Buy American." "Develop energy independence." "Subsidize American steel."

For a Christian, patriotism always has its limits. We need to be aware of when our quality of life is sustained at the expense of the workers of other countries of the world. We need to assure that no economic institution accrues such power that it cannot be held accountable for its deeds. We need to know the difference between saying that "Small is beautiful" and opposing growth that contributes to the common good.

I have indicated some of the sophisticated quandaries that face the thoughtful Christian in making sense in our day of the economic implications of the Gospel. The individual person may or may not have specific training in these areas.

But a position of leadership and service in the community demands that we learn as much as we can and engage in the process of collective discernment that keeps the community of faith helpful to its members seeking wisdom for their daily lives.

Business ethics is a growth discipline in contemporary Church life. The range of issues is so vast that I have been able to focus on only a few. I hope that I have struck a responsive chord, forced you to recall some forgotten incident or present experience of conflict. We are called to be a "light to the world." We are simply, in one sense, Christians earning a living by the sweat of our brows. Yet our presence in the workplace should make a difference.

In all of our concrete work situations, we can suffer from failure, boredom, and routine. Even cocreators can lose a proper perspective on the value of what they do. For this reason, we need to be reminded that it is the pooled labor of all our minds, hands, and hearts that, in God's good time, will bring the Kingdom to its longed-for completion.

A Harvest of Questions: Chemicals and the Food Chain

I do not approach the subject of chemicals and food as a scold, nor with any particular position to advocate. As an ethicist, I have spent a good deal of time investigating the relationships between various fields of expertise and the development of public policy. Looking at the issue from that perspective, I hope not so much to suggest answers to the many questions encompassed by this topic as to illuminate what is at stake in these deliberations, how broad is their impact and how important their ultimate outcome.

Three recent cases can serve as reference points in this discussion: In the aftermath of the controversy over alar and apples, the impression one has is that we have moved from a situation in which, at any time during the year, we could be guaranteed a product that *looked* healthy to a situation in which that guarantee of appearance no longer exists, but in which the reality may be healthier apples.

In the second case, the so-called Chilean grape scare, virtually all of that country's fruit and produce were removed from the market because of the detection of a couple of grapes that seemed to be contaminated. The cost to Chile's economy was many hundred millions of dollars. This raises the question not so much of goodwill, but rather of proportionality. Was this response—which could be repeated under similar circumstances in the future—a good and proper one? What motivated it and is there any lesson to be learned from the controversy?

More recently, and with less heat and hysteria, the relationship of oat bran to cholesterol has been the subject of debate. In background materials on this subject, the point is made that our nation could significantly and relatively easily increase production of oats. But in light of the questioning of oat bran's value, is increased production necessary or desirable anymore?

In each of these cases there seems to be an almost instantaneous relationship between the communication of information, controversy, and public response. This we have to live with, but what about the larger question that encompasses all these cases—the question of health and public policy? Here are a few overall observations on the subject.

First, generally in this country, particularly in the twentieth century, the strength of our medicine has been its therapeutic rather than its preventive capabilities. Our medical schools and our central medical research facilities are the envy of much of the world, yet in some parts of the world with less investment in so-called high-tech medicine and where less is expected of medical care after the diagnosis of disease, considerably more attention is paid to prevention.

Second, ours is an aging population with a greater concern over illnesses such as cancer and problems of the heart than is the case in those areas of the world where people die younger. This certainly influences our attitudes and responses to cancer and to anything suspected of increasing the risk of this disease.

Third, health care costs are escalating at a rate much higher than inflation. This fact is prompting increasing discussion of public policy alternatives and increasing experimentation in health care delivery. One example has been the seesaw debate over catastrophic health care. Another is the intense competition among health care providers. Not all of them are going to survive. Which will, and what will be the standard of care?

Fourth, an educated population has access to frequent media programming which addresses questions of health and health care. If one subscribes to cable television which has a channel devoted twenty-four hours a day to health issues, occasionally one will see it even if it is not one's primary choice for viewing. Others may spend hours during the week watching whatever appears. How does this frequent exposure to information—some of it exaggerated or premature—alter our expectations of what science and technology can provide, e.g., the perfect baby, the ideal way to die? How old do we expect to be when we die, and how healthy do we expect to be as we approach the end? One objection to living wills is that most people, as they grow older, change their minds concerning how much ill health they are willing to tolerate. Our psychology is influenced, among other things, by what we see as our possibilities at different stages in our lives.

All of this is background to considering the question of cancer. Is there anyone who does not share some part of the fear of this mysterious disease? What is its origin? What is the likely prognosis if we or those close to us are diagnosed as having some form of cancer? Is there not a kind of onco-genic paranoia among us such that whenever the big "C" is mentioned, the collective national psyche reacts. Just as with the anti-drug effort, in which I am involved, cancer research and experimentation are termed a "war," which leads many among the public to believe that the solution of the problem is simply a matter of will and commitment and conviction.

But maybe cancer is not like that. Maybe it won't go away. Maybe there is not a cure, because it is more than one thing. Debate rages on the relative impact of genetic and environmental factors. What do we do with this thing which remains so mysterious in the eyes of the public? So many individuals and so many families have been affected, and even when there is remission, still the concern lingers that something "out there"—something related perhaps to my or others' actions—will, in the long run, have some kind of detrimental effect.

Another observation concerning health and public policy is that the public is suspicious of regulatory bureaucracy. This particularly affects the roles played by the Environmental Protection Agency (EPA) and the Food and Drug Administration (FDA). Certainly President Reagan struck a nerve when he campaigned against the over-bureaucratization of government. Since then, many candidates at the state and local levels have claimed that, if elected, they were going to get back to basics. Very seldom does that happen. Why is that? Is it simply the iron wall of bureaucracy or does the complexity of modern life demand that we increasingly subdivide responsibilities for various aspects of our lives? Speaking specifically about EPA—and on behalf of the general public—I must ask, what is the governmental mandate of EPA? Is it clear and well defined? Does the agency operate in a spirit of consensus and confidence? What resources does it require to fulfill its responsibilities properly? What degree of relative immunity should it enjoy from political pressures? (Of course, such pressures come with the air we breathe, but there are means of removing key people from the firing line and keeping them a step removed from the most recent controversy.) All of these considerations must be taken into account in critiquing EPA or any agency; it is unfair to levy broadsides with no sense of what is necessary for an agency to function properly.

There are, I would suggest, two sharply contrasting tendencies in contemporary American life relative to health and public policy, and we can probably see them in our own lives as well. On the one hand, we have developed a keener collective sense of personal responsibility for health—a greater consciousness of the need for exercise, a good diet, adequate sleep and relaxation to relieve stress. This consciousness has produced significant changes among our people. Recall your 25th, 30th, or 40th class reunion. My experience has been that you now can divide your friends and acquaintances into two categories—those who look healthy and those who do not. In past generations, by contrast, I suspect there was only one such category at reunions—those who looked older. This trend does not mean that all is well, but I do think we are seeing people accepting greater responsibility for their own lives and health.

There is, however, the countertrend I mentioned, namely the persistence of certain unsafe practices—cigarette smoking, the excessive consumption of alcohol, the abuse of drugs whether for recreation or performance enhancement, and the increasing incidence of sexually transmitted diseases. How do we account for these trends existing side by side? In seeking to answer questions of health and public policy, in seeking to chart alternative courses of action and develop persuasive policy recommendations, we must take into account these puzzling twin trends and consider how best to encourage the one while discouraging the other.

Let me move now to a second dimension of this issue and three brief thought experiments. The first concerns the fluoridation of drinking water. Judging as a lay person, I think there is overwhelming evidence of the beneficial results of the fluoridation of water. (This evidence includes the closing of dental schools on university campuses across the country.) It seems a proven fact that the introduction of this chemical into the drinking water enhances dental health. And yet there still are many communities in this country in which fluoridation of water is so divisive a political topic that to introduce it is unthinkable.

What does this phenomenon tell us?

The second thought experiment concerns chemotherapy. Chemotherapy and radiation treatment often are comparable ways of treating cancer, and both basically involve the poisoning of the human body to destroy and prevent the spread of cancerous cells. In return for a hoped-for cure, we agree to tolerate certain severe side effects; we damage or destroy the part to save the whole, a bargain not too dissimilar from certain kinds of surgery. Of course, chemotherapy is not something people enter into enthusiastically; they do it under duress and medical advice because it seems a lesser evil than the alternatives.

What does this tell us about attitudes concerning health and the introduction of hazardous substances into the body?

A third thought experiment concerns biotechnological intervention. The Florida citrus crop, especially in north Florida, was badly damaged by severe weather in December 1989—the second time that had happened in the past four or five years. During that same period, efforts had been made in California to use biotechnological intervention to experiment with frost resistant crops. These attempts had been opposed by various community interest groups out of the fear of unforeseen side effects. It seems to me that the future will demand more reflection on such matters. We will need to find the proper balance between protecting the quality of food products at a minimum cost to the environment and utilizing human creativity and technological intervention to maximize the availability of these same products.

Fluoridation of water, chemotherapy, biotechnological intervention—all offer ways to rethink the question of chemical use versus food and health. At the same time, our scientists and researchers must be willing to acknowledge that their work is inherently ambiguous and that portraying all scientific development as beneficial to humanity flies in the face of history.

Is this true of medicine? We have discovered the existence of iatrogenic diseases or conditions. In the very attempt to help someone, even in hospital conditions, some percentage of people are harmed and may even die. There is no guarantee that medicine is as much an art as it is a science. And from the past, the revelations of the Nuremburg trials concerning Nazi medicine are a chilling reminder of the evil that can be done when science is misused.

In transportation, society tolerates thousands of deaths in auto accidents each year for the sake of speed and convenience. People worry about air travel, which statistically is one of the safest things we do, yet think nothing of driving thousands of miles each year in a car, where we are far more likely to die.

Science offers us tools for the enrichment of the human mind and spirit, yet there are side effects that we need to evaluate. This is true of communications. We can have a billion cable networks. What is going to be on them? We can have videos and VCRs everywhere; what is going to be watched? What is it that pleases us aesthetically? How can the packaging of information lead to wisdom? We must recall the warning of computer scientists—"garbage in; garbage out." We must recognize that the simple development of a technique or a technology in and of itself is not sufficient.

Energy is another example. The relative impacts of fossil fuels and nuclear energy on human life and well-being have been debated at great length. This debate illustrates again the ambiguity of science and technology and that there can be no such thing as a value-free science. Max Weber long ago, and Thomas Kuhn more recently, have persuasively made this case. There is in science a continuing search for objectivity. There is a reciprocity between the questions we ask and the answers we are open to at any given moment. In that sense, the scientific method is one of the great achievements of the human mind and spirit—a way of moving beyond our prejudices, our biases and our close-mindedness. It helps us to understand more fully the natural order (whatever that may be), human nature and the dynamics of human society.

But there is nothing inevitable about the wise use of what we learn through science. This is why interdisciplinary cooperation can help us all to understand better the limitations, the risks, the dilemmas posed by the knowledge we unearth within our own areas of specialization. The temptation to hyperspecialization can divorce us from concern over the wider consequences of what we are doing. If we work in a company, we only touch a part of the overall effort. If we work in a university, there is only so much that we can do at a given moment. We may never comprehend or even recognize the significance of what is being done around us. All of us, I believe, need to come to a greater awareness of the consequences for humankind of science and technology. The question of values persists because it is only in terms of the values we prize and are committed to that we can hope to resolve complex issues such as those involved in the relationships of chemicals and food.

Ethics really is about values, about their normative status, and the evaluation of specific actions or policies in terms of some hierarchy of values. Is survival or the quality of life more important? It all depends. For those unable to survive, quality of life is meaningless. Some people live hand to mouth, we say. Will there be food on the table tomorrow? Who knows? Spend some time in Bangladesh or India or Brazil among the poorest of the poor. They are not concerned with questions of food additives. They simply want bread for themselves and their families. They want something rather than nothing, yet that does not—and should not—prevent us from asking questions about the quality of life.

What about justice and love or peace and security? On some issues we recognize that values conflict and that we must choose where we stand, what our goals are, and what style of life best leads to happiness for ourselves or others. Reality is richer, deeper, fuller than a purely empirical perspective allows for. There is myth—for example, Icarus flying with wax wings and coming too close to the sun. What is Icarus about? What does this myth tell us about the attempt to probe and explore the unknown? Is it worth it? Presumably, he died. There is Prometheus, stealing fire from the gods and suffering eternal punishment. There is Dr. Faustus bargaining with the devil to endow his life in this world with greater knowledge and understanding. There is Dr. Frankenstein with his monster or the universe of Star Wars with its "droids" and all the images that has created for contemporary life. There is also the symbolic level. What about kosher foods? To some the notion seems crazy. Why do people do that? Because it goes back to some deeply held dimension of a religious heritage and tradition. What about sacred animals? Another religious tradition refuses to eat certain animals because of the high regard in which they are held. To kill and to eat such animals, these people insist, would be a destruction of self, that is, the very antithesis of nutrition. Fasting and abstaining from meat are promoted in many traditions as holy acts, forms of religious discipline intended to prompt a keener recognition of how easily we can be driven by bodily need alone. There is also, in my tradition and others, the sacred meal, like any meal only given a worth beyond what is immediately apparent to the senses.

The mythic level, the symbolic level, and the empirical level all are part of reality as we experience it. If we reduce this reality simply to what is visible and testable, we miss recognizing the full human dimension of how people approach specific issues—what is affecting me in my food or in the air or in the cigarette smoke of the person sitting on the airplane, and how do I respond to it? What am I looking for from these genies that I let escape from the bottle? Public policy results from a recognition of the proper and human use of science and technology tested by the values that we defend as individuals and as members of a community.

I make three claims. First, public policy must respect and take account of the perspectives and values of the various communities that make up the nation, i.e., in a democratic society with a pluralism of values we need to discern, to listen, and to try to build consensus.

Second, it is difficult to forge conceptual language that clarifies complex issues and contributes to reaching a consensus. We must try, even though not everyone likes the development of conceptual languages. Think, for example, what it means to say that one is pro-life or pro-choice—the passion and deep feeling built into the terminology. This is true of almost every issue. I am pro-environment; I am pro-natural order; I am pro-intervention, because it will allow human life to be better. The language we use is often a weapon rather than a means of clarification.

Third, peer review for scientists, government boards, institutional review boards and the like, while sometimes cumbersome and slow, is essential to protect the common good. This is a vote of confidence for process, despite those who would say it delays good and necessary actions.

Finally, what about the use of chemical pesticides and other such substances in agriculture? The goal of such use is a simple one—to maximize yield of high quality fruits and vegetables at minimum cost to both growers and consumers and with minimum health risk to growers, harvesters, packagers and consumers. What are the problems? One is significant slippage in consumer confidence, a slippage that is exacerbated by adverse publicity. A second problem is open debate about risk assessment. Scientists and others do not agree about risk assessment and therefore the public is confused. "When will the so-called experts make up their minds?" "Who will furnish the overview to resolve the differences of opinion?" So asks the public. A third problem is what some have called the Delaney paradox—that we have sometimes contradictory federal regulations. A fourth problem is the question of concomitant risk, not simply residues and their toxic effects on consumers of fruits and vegetables, but also exposure of workers, impact on wildlife, contamination of ground water which could have an impact on great numbers of people. And the last problem is the inability of government agencies under any possible scenario to monitor more than a small fraction of the food supply.

At least four possible resolutions of these problems suggest themselves. One is to focus on the process of risk assessment. The claim is made that herbicides are relatively low-risk chemicals, that insecticides occupy the middle range, and that fungicides are higher risk and therefore ought to be the subject of greater attention. Does that allow the direction of public policy and debate to concentrate on those chemical substances that are higher risk? If so, it does not eliminate the question of overall risk assessment, but it is one possible avenue of resolution. A second possible resolution: Is there a viable consensus on what constitutes a negligible risk standard? Is the one in one million level too strict, too lenient, or an accurate gauge? In any matter of public policy and government regulation, a clear standard that everyone can agree upon makes for much easier development of understanding and support. A third possible resolution: What about alternative agriculture? Is it just a short list of specific strategies or is it a philosophy of farming, a philosophy of life? Is alternative agriculture a kind of utopian appeal to the few? Realistically, could it be adopted in this country or abroad by the vast majority of farmers? Finally, a resolution has been proposed, and may eventually be achieved by biotechnological development. Is it possible to develop new strains? Is it possible that what is now simply promised will lead to early tests and eventually to wide-scale use by producers?

Whatever the answers to these questions, continued public debate is crucial. The formulation of public policy in a democracy requires a prudential judgment and a balancing of competing values. So-called pure positions—those which are internally coherent and consistent—are seldom possible. We all live with uncertainty; we change our minds periodically about what direction is best. In that sense, we do not have pure positions, so continuing research and debate is essential both to clarify our current situation and to suggest alternatives for the future.

Two images with which to conclude: In the Catholic community, the Gospel reading for today is the parable of the sower. Jesus tells of the sower throwing seed—as was typical at that time. Some seed fell by the side of the road and was eaten by the birds, some fell on rocky soil and did not take root, some fell in the midst of thorns that eventually crushed it, and some fell on good soil. The religious interpretation of the parable goes in other directions, but it is interesting to think of it in terms of the goals of chemical intervention in agriculture. Is it to allow the seed that falls on rocky or thorn-filled ground to survive, or is it to enable the seed that falls on good ground to yield a harvest many times greater than ever before?

The second image is from the Garden of Eden. Whether one takes that as a literal, historical account or as a metaphor, the Garden represents an idyllic period before human history. From the perspective of that setting, what would be the relationship between human knowledge, human intervention, and the productivity of the fields? Is there anything inherently bad or destructive or contaminating in the use of what we know under controlled conditions by those who care deeply about the well-being of the human family?

We need food and drink to survive and flourish as human persons. We would like that food and drink to be healthy for us and we would like to maintain our health for a reasonable span of years.

The controversies and the debates concerning the use of chemicals in agriculture ultimately are healthy steps leading us in the direction, not of trying to recapture some Garden of Eden, but of making sense of our options in the real world. May we recognize that responsibility and engage it openly and well.

The Control of Violence,
Foreign and Domestic:
Some Ethical Lessons
from Law Enforcement

What social scientist can claim to have known what was going to happen in Russia, in Eastern Europe, in Chile, in Afghanistan, in Namibia, or any of the other places in the world that have recently experienced radical change? Who had an overview sufficient to incorporate the tremendous variety of social, political, and economic circumstances that exist in our world today and make accurate predictions? Much is unknown, but I feel there are certain claims that we can safely make.

It is probable that we will see a continuation of smaller-scale conflicts: Think of what has happened or is happening in Ethiopia, Cambodia, Lebanon, Angola, El Salvador, Yugoslavia, and many other similar places. We have also seen the expansion of terrorism, and the capacity of dedicated and well-financed groups to gain access to the high technology and its instruments of destruction. This, no doubt, will continue to be a serious problem. We will most probably continue to face narcotics traffickers, in a sense, taking over legitimate governments, corrupting them from within, and having the economic power of multinational corporations. As a response to that, both the military and law enforcement agencies will be asked to undertake roles for which they have no specific training or expertise. In tight budgetary times, false promises can be made in order to keep up morale and personnel numbers. For the foreseeable future, the military and federal law enforcement agencies will be under great pressure to prove that they can combat international terrorist organizations and drug cartels as effectively as the armies of the Soviet Union or interstate bank robbers.

The Roman Catholic tradition is committed to a broader frame of reference relative to war and peace. Called the just war theory, it dates from the Greco-Roman period and was adapted and modified through the ages by various representatives of particularly, though not exclusively, the Christian tradition. The just war theory provides a way of analyzing the context of the morality of war and the exercise and use of violence. Certain well-established criteria have emerged in this analysis.

The criterion of *legitimate authority* states that war cannot be declared arbitrarily or by the whim or fancy of a few, but must be prepared for—and promulgated by—a legitimately established government. It must be for a *just cause*, often described in terms of national defense. It must take place as a *last resort*, that is, only after every effort has been expended to keep it from happening. (This recognizes the terrible human tragedy that accompanies the making of war.) It must be under *right intention*: Each person who prepares for or participates in the conflict must have prepared himself or herself in terms of the moral scheme of things, thinking through what is acceptable and appropriate and what is not, being prepared to say *no* even when that is an unpopular decision. (And we know that the momentum of events and the difficulty of ascertaining facts in the midst of conflict makes all of this difficult.)

Much of just war theory in the twentieth-century has
been devoted to reflection about the fifth criterion, *moral
means*. Because of the scale and destructive capability of
our weaponry, because of the integrated nature of modern
life where very seldom are military forces isolated from the
civilian populations, we have had to undertake an analysis of forms of fighting, the very legitimacy of which is in
question. In discussing the question of moral means, three
governing principles have been developed. The principle of
discrimination, or noncombatant immunity, traces its origins
to the beginning of the Greco-Roman period and has been a
constant feature of the analysis over the last 2,000 years. This
considers the distinction that must be made between those
who can be legitimately described as the enemy—those who
bear arms against our side—and the civilian population. But
we know, looking back on the first and second World Wars,
on Korea, on Vietnam, and on many smaller-scale conflicts,
that maintaining this distinction is extremely difficult. We
have creeping into our language the notion of "collateral
damage," when some percentage of civilians are put at risk
because there is no other way of winning in a particular kind
of engagement.

The second principle we have placed under the rubric of
moral means is the principle of *proportionality*. Common
sense dictates that we should not enter a war that we cannot
win. In addition to that, as human beings who can exercise
our intelligence and weigh and evaluate things, we should
seek to participate in only such conflicts wherein, all things
being equal and acceptable, a greater good will result than
the evil that will be suffered. But this is difficult to evaluate,
not simply in the short term, in terms of body count, but also
in the long term, in the perpetuating of hostility and hatred.

The final principle derived from moral means is that of
humane treatment—to respect the dignity of the enemy,
however difficult that may be. Examples of this principle
can be found in the treatment of prisoners, the immunity of

those who are serving as medics, ambassadors, or negotiators with the other side, and in trying to preserve certain other civilized practices in war that developed in the Middle Ages and that have been incorporated into the statutes of international law. These three subscripts to the general criterion of moral means are flexible in their applications, and like the other general criteria of the just war theory, are designed as creative ways to help us think through the questions of morality in war.

Now let us consider what it means to be a professional. Becoming a professional requires, first of all, specialized training. One must acquire a broad general background, develop a technical expertise appropriate to the discipline, and master a certain set of principles before one is able to competently practice a profession. Second, there is invariably some sort of certification. At the end of the training program, the professional body, or those otherwise involved in the profession, must in a sense confirm that one has accomplished all that is required; only then is one inducted into the profession. Third, in the training and also in the early periods of practice, the inculcation of a code or set of values or way of thinking about moral responsibility as a professional person is an essential part of any profession. Finally, a profession usually conveys status and/or a higher than usual level of financial reward. Being held in high regard mirrors what we discover when doing surveys of popular opinion. What would young children like to be? In answer, the professions are normally clumped near the top of the pecking order—but that can change. After certain kinds of scandals are given public exposure in a given profession, its status commonly suffers. All of this suggests that being a professional carries with it high levels of expectation placed upon one by the public one is committed to serve.

It is the third characteristic I find most interesting for this discussion: the unique moral responsibilities we claim to carry as professionals. We are all familiar with the Hippocratic Oath. Whether it is directly the conviction of the Greek

philosopher Hippocrates or not, it has a long-standing significance in the way members of the medical profession think
about themselves, the quintessentially professional convictions they have about themselves and the patients entrusted
to their care. The oath codifies an attitude of service and the
receipt of a solemn trust. For example, it expresses concern
about confidentiality, about protecting information that one
gains in a privileged context so as not to abuse what has been
entrusted. For a profession to be a profession in the sense
of which we are speaking (vis-à-vis merely taking money for
one's services), this element of trust and service to the client
or society is indispensable. The codes that we find in the
various professions simply make this attitude explicit.

Perhaps the most difficult task for a professional person
and for the profession as a whole is enforcing the code. The
Air Force Academy has an honor code. We at Notre Dame
had one, abandoned it, and are in the process of trying to
revive it. Our experience has been that there is one major
factor that makes an honor code difficult to implement in the
college environment: In the end, nobody is comfortable turning someone else in. They may espouse the value, they may
even live by it themselves, but it is quite another matter, a
much more difficult task, to hold a peer accountable. Nobody
likes a whistle blower; nobody likes somebody who seems
self-righteous or cannot respect the limitations of human
nature and human weakness. Yet for a profession to be held
in consistently high regard, the willingness to hold others
accountable must be present.

The problem is not peculiar to any particular profession
and might be found in medicine, law, the military, law enforcement, or teaching. I have observed it in the many facets
of my professional life as well. Unfortunately, most of us
have had some occasion to see teachers who are ill prepared,
professors who are incompetent for one reason or another.
No one wants to hold them accountable, fearing that the
profession as a whole will be tainted. Yet the result of this
inaction and rationalization is that, over time, the profession

indeed is tainted and the level of trust broken down. It is estimated that 20 percent of the physicians in this country have a problem with some type of substance abuse. At the very least, this would lead one to become more wary about medical care since its practitioners have such easy access to drugs. Clearly, one ought to recognize that when a few are incompetent, the whole profession suffers.

In light of these comments on the professions in general, I would like to focus on ethics as applied to law enforcement and test out the workability of just war theory. In some ways law enforcement is a more controlled setting than is a military operation in wartime. We can look at what the difficulties are and why the profession is more or less successful in facing certain dilemmas. I will take a theory that most people apply primarily to war and peace and reduce it to the more manageable scale of the ethics of law enforcement.

Prior to 1829, there were not any police as we know them today. There were constables, sheriffs, and watchmen, who were generally uneducated and ill prepared for the role assigned to them. One of the first police forces was established, at least indirectly, because gin was introduced into England. Gin, distilled as a way of reducing the surplus of corn, created a terrible problem of alcohol abuse in London and other English cities. Responding to the resulting violence and other crime, Sir Robert Peale took the initiative in establishing a group that could ensure safety in English cities. The word "bobbies" comes from his first name. From the days of Peale until the present, we have seen in most countries of Europe and North America a multiplicity of police agencies, some 40,000 in this country alone.

Law enforcement agencies have had a difficult time dealing with professionalization. Right up to the present, the very desirability of professionalizing the police has been debated in various public policy journals. In order to attract the very best people to this crucial work, agencies have paid great attention to the recruitment and selection process, to police training, and to better pay scales.

There still, however, remains a question as to whether or not police officers should be college-educated, and this question must be settled before law enforcement at all levels can be compared to the professional model we outlined earlier. Certification to practice is also an unsettled issue. Should there be lateral entry? Should one be able to move from a police force in Chicago to another in Denver? Today, this is not generally done, excepting transfers at the very top level. More typically, the police live a relatively isolated existence, spending their entire careers in one place. This is very different from other professions, where, for example, lawyers or doctors can take certification examinations in a state other than where they received their professional training. There is a kind of transferability. I would argue that, because of the complexity and the central significance of the law enforcement function, its practice should be more thoroughly professionalized, with a great deal more attention paid to recruitment, selection, training, certification and perhaps most important, the inculcation and enforcement of a code.

One of the most significant things about law enforcement that demands professionalization, and distinguishes it from military service, is police discretion. By *discretion* I mean the breadth of choice, the leeway in decision making, given to the individual officer. We can see that police discretion calls for a greater degree of professionalization at the lowest levels, since the officer on the beat is making most of the basic decisions as to what constitutes crime, when to enforce a particular law, what to charge a suspect with, and what procedures to follow in arrests and evidence gathering— procedures that could gain or lose a conviction.

It is interesting, too, to note that police discretion is a necessary and unavoidable feature of law enforcement, because it is impossible for the police to enforce all the laws all the time. Homicide and narcotics investigators, for example, cannot waste time enforcing parking and traffic regulations. At the same time police agencies tend to be selective, depending upon the signals they receive from their constituencies. For instance, laws against gambling or prostitution might be ignored in response to implicit signals from the political leadership.

Decisions like these are made all the time, and the use of discretion varies not only from one law enforcement agency to another, but also within the larger departments, from one precinct or area to another. Surely the potential for abuse lies here, as in, for example, prejudicial enforcement: more severe enforcement against inner-city blacks than suburban whites, more severe enforcement against young males in general than against older people, less enforcement against white collar crime than against crimes committed by the less fortunate, and so on. Besides being manifestly unfair, prejudicial law enforcement has the pernicious effect of breeding disrespect for the law.

There are other types of selective enforcement, such as the various categories of immunity. A system in which information is obtained from informants can also mean that a full-time burglar might never go to jail if he or she provides evidence in narcotics or rape cases. The fairness of this system is, of course, a separate issue, with its own set of accompanying problems. Still, we are all at least casually acquainted with the system and for the most part, are used to the arrangement.

Another form of selective enforcement involves the revival of antiquated laws. An individual officer knowledgeable about such laws might enforce, say, a "quiet law" that has not been in use for more than fifty years in order to clear downtown streets of so-called "undesirables," who otherwise are doing nothing wrong.

The necessities and difficulties associated with discretion in law enforcement give us something to think about in terms of the way the military functions, particularly with regard to the use of violence. Comparing the two provides a rich topic for discussion. Is discretion distributed optimally in the military structure? Could military command structures be modified to gain some of the advantages inherent in the way the police use discretion? Are the exercises of discretion in the military, wherever that authority might ultimately lie, subject to the same sorts of temptation to abuse this power or exercise it incompetently? If little or no discretion is available to the individual in the military, how much calling into account is appropriate when mistakes are made by those in command? All of these questions related to discretion should be addressed when discussing the nature of the military or indeed, of any profession.

In this country, police are armed and are trained in the use of force. They have discretion in both the use of force and the kind of force used—handcuffs, tear gas, pistols, shot guns, automatic weapons, etc. We all have seen the comparisons of our police with those in England and other parts of the world where generally the officer on the beat is not armed. Are our police officers armed because of our fascination with firearms, our "wild west" syndrome? Or does it have to do with fears that once firearms are available to criminals, law enforcement agents must have them to enforce the law? Whatever the historical origins or justifications, I think it foolish to entertain the idea of adopting a police system like that in England. We live in circumstances where normally our police officers will be armed, as those properly trained on the Notre Dame security force are armed (though I know of no instance in our school's history where those firearms have been used). Given an armed police force, then, a force exercising a high degree of discretionary authority, the criteria of just war theory now becomes applicable to law enforcement.

First, with regard to *legitimate authority*, the police officer can only validly use coercive force when he or she, in fact, represents the body politic. In some parts of the world police death squads, or so-called right wing death squads, exercise deadly force outside the legitimate political machinery: "We can't get them legitimately, so we'll get them illegitimately." That is simply unacceptable within our constitutional tradition, no less within our standards of right and wrong, as is any use of force by the police for personal vendettas. Legitimate authority, then, suggests a control over the exercise of violence by law enforcement agents.

Second, with regard to *just cause*, the police should have written guidelines for the use of guns, mace, choke holds, and all the other means of constraining or harming another person. The discretion of the individual officer must be exercised only within the constraints of this established code. This is only to say that law enforcement needs a code as the military needs a code, as clerics need a code, as teachers need a code.

The criterion of *last resort* in the context of law enforcement means that the police should exhaust all possible methods for controlling a situation before resorting to the more severe levels of force. One of the most difficult circumstances that law enforcement agents can face is domestic violence. Entering a household, police find a husband and wife, sometimes parents and children, fighting; sometimes there are weapons. Often, as soon as an intervention takes place, family members turn against the officer. The question of the appropriate use of force or style of interaction requires a high level of training; more and more, there are—and need to be—specialists for this kind of situation, as for potential suicides and hostage takers.

If they are acting from *right intention*, police will use the full force available to them only when they are convinced that the common good is being served, not for personal safety alone or because of some high level of emotional response. In certain military engagements, verbal provocation or the witnessing of horrendous acts can precipitate a breakdown of restraint. The same is true in law enforcement when, perhaps in the course of an arrest, suspects resort to verbal or physical provocation. Restraint in such situations—acting from an intention to enforce the law, not to respond to insults—requires a level of training and self-control that exemplifies why both the military and law enforcement ideally should be professions.

Under the criterion of *moral means*, we can find examples of all three subordinate principles, i.e., discrimination, proportionality, and humane treatment. Police use of force must never be indiscriminate, that is, directed at groups of people in general. We demand this of the police, even when it is difficult, as in mass demonstrations. We all can recall in our own lifetimes vivid examples of indiscriminate use of force, such as the march on Selma, Alabama, where the official mass hostility of the police was the direct cause of violence and injury. The principle of discrimination also calls for considering seriously the impact specific force will have on the innocent. When, for example, can tear gas be used and what about hot pursuit? There is nothing more frustrating for a law enforcement agent in a car chasing a felon than to abandon the chase because of the risk to pedestrians and other motorists, but when the risk to innocents is real, the principle of discrimination requires that restraint be exercised. The same is true with kidnapping, skyjackings, and other crimes involving innocent bystanders. To exercise restraint because too many lives are at stake is to recognize that people of good will, who try to do the right thing, will sometimes have to refrain from doing what would otherwise be right because of the potential impact on others.

The principle of proportionality calls for weighing the good and evil results of an action or policy in both the short and the long term. Applying it to a hypothetical firearms policy, how much discretionary authority should an officer have in the discharge of his or her weapon? What sort of weapons ought he or she to have? Most police agencies today prohibit the use of warning shots simply to capture a suspect because of the risk inherent in firing a weapon; the risk involved is disproportionate to the task at hand. Still, it is very difficult to maintain this principle when officers' lives are at stake. Similarly, when a police officer does use a gun, the prime intention should be to incapacitate rather than to kill the suspect. That is, there is no general warrant for deadly force in every case where it may be legitimate to use a weapon. Once again, there are difficulties maintaining this principle, especially today in some drug cases because of the firepower available to the dealers, because of the brazenness with which certain dealers operate, and because of the desperation law enforcement agents often feel in fighting what they perceive as a losing battle.

For all these reasons, in every instance where a police officer fires a gun in the line of duty, there should be a full investigation by responsible representatives of the people, some kind of civilian review board. Of course, few police officers would like that; they would take it as an affront to their trustworthiness and their internal departmental procedures. Several years ago in New York City there were eighteen incidents in which civilians were killed or seriously wounded by police. Perhaps every one of those instances was a legitimate exercise of force in a violent society, but perhaps not. In this or similar situations the police leadership may be too inexperienced or too embarrassed to review properly or to respond to these incidents, and the inclination to tolerate them, which we discussed previously, is invariably present. Credibility is indispensable for a profession and for its members. A civilian review board is a way to gain that credibility, particularly if those who serve on it have the confidence of the public.

Again applying the principle of proportionality, it seems obvious that the type of weapon and ammunition police officers are allowed to carry while on duty should be, and in most agencies is, clearly specified in departmental regulations. The power of the revolver or automatic weapon, the kind of ammunition, the use of concealed weapons, and other weapons considerations must be tailored to the situation at hand. Proportionality dictates that different responses are appropriate in different situations. Certainly undercover officers routinely could be called upon to use different levels and types of force than police on patrol. Another example of the need for different responses is riot control. Police must be trained to recognize the difference between normal patrol duty where a high level of discretion is called for and group confrontations where strict obedience to the chain of command is most effective. In riots police should probably become more like the military; conversely, when the National Guard or other military units are called to riot control duty, they must act like police agencies rather than as troops engaging in warfare.

Riot control illustrates another aspect of proportionality: Decisions on the form and levels of force employed in group confrontations should always be based on the priority of persons over property. That is particularly problematic when such things as looting or arson are taking place. After Martin Luther King, Jr., was killed, I was in Washington, trapped on 14th Street N.W. in the midst of a riot. People were throwing rocks through my windshield, and the car stalled out. I finally got it started and, filled with fear, beat a hasty retreat, driving down a city street at what seemed to be 80 mph. I had this sense of chaos and that everything was out of control. Under those circumstances it was easy to recognize why it can be so difficult to place the lives and welfare of people first and how easy it can be to respond disproportionately.

It also is essential that we view proportionality in terms of human dignity, which should include respect for privacy. Electronic surveillance should be prohibited; that is, private detectives, business competitors, and others should never have the authority to conduct that kind of surveillance. Only those properly certified by the government should have such power. Electronic surveillance by the police and other law enforcement agencies should only be done with explicit court approval; that is, there should be no blanket permissions. Privacy rights must be foremost in these circumstances, although certain kinds of criminal activity may be controllable only by surveillance techniques. A balance must be struck between the evil produced by the means employed (that is, violations of legitimate privacy rights) and the good resulting from these enforcement techniques.

Finally, there is the principle of humane treatment. What kind of application does it have to law enforcement? Certainly it is applicable to interrogation methods. The use of torture as a means of interrogation, for example, is never justified. Yet I have had debates in my classes with students who do not accept that principle. They offer up all sorts of hypotheticals in attempts to support their positions, but I see this issue as one of the great test cases of our attitude about the dignity of the human person. Torture that we deem unacceptable is administered all over the world by regimes of the left, the right, and sometimes the center. We have no difficulty in condemning them, yet we entertain all too easily scenarios that might legitimize our own use of torture. In law enforcement, a confession often is seen as crucial in making a case, yet there is very little evidence of that in court records; in fact, a confession often gets in the way of a conviction because of the way it was obtained or because of the legal controversies that surround it. For both moral and purely instrumental considerations, procedures of interrogation should place maximum emphasis on the rights of the accused.

To conclude, I have five summary comments. First, professional life for all of us presupposes training, certification, a professional code involving moral and professional standards and the courage to enforce them, and the trust and respect of the clients or society we serve. Professional life begins in the training, and that is why honor codes are so crucial—they test the character of those who aspire to membership in the profession. The hardest part of a code, the hardest part of being part of a profession, is enforcing the code—-enforcing it in our own lives and, with even more difficulty, applying it to our fellow professionals.

Second, just war theory is an attempt to approach morally the great human problem of violence and its control. We all wish that violence would go away, we all wish that we lived in a more peaceful and just world, but it is not that way. We struggle as moral beings relative to our religious and cultural heritages to find a set of guidelines to help us think through the challenges that we face. Just war theory is a powerful and flexible framework for that purpose and will serve us well if we will use it.

Third, just war theory is more readily applicable to law enforcement practices than to modern military engagements. This is largely a function of scale and the ability to control the level of violence and the number of participants. But the same fundamental values are at stake in both situations.

Fourth, realize that personal integrity is a quest rather than an achievement. A person of character will seek to do the right thing for the right reason and will also admit mistakes or errors of judgment when they occur. It is not simply what we profess, it is not simply trying with all of our might to achieve a life of integrity. It is also being willing to admit our mistakes, publicly when that is called for, but more importantly, privately, in the innermost recesses of our hearts.

Finally, the proper exercise of leadership within a profession calls forth all that is best and most risky in the human condition. Knowledge and prior reflection must be wedded to courage and patient resolve. Our nation and our world need such leadership, today more than ever before.

PART THREE

*Challenges within
the University*

The University and Cultural Progress

While "change" is inevitable and constant in human affairs (if only because we and the institutions we establish are immersed in space and time), "progress" is not. A retrospective look at the twentieth century with its high-technology wars, death toll on the highways, and degradation of the environment would suggest an inherent ambiguity in all human activity and that those who in the past promised that "things are getting better and better" were either blind, deaf, or deliberately naive.

I do not want to suggest that progress has not been made, but rather that we need to be critical in the midst of inflated claims and ideological promises. We have seen in the last year or two phenomenal sociopolitical changes—in Eastern Europe and the USSR, in Chile and Nicaragua, in Namibia and South Africa. Yet each of these stories is incomplete and the peoples of these and other societies still have many choices to make. Our world has become so interdependent, economically and culturally, that no nation, no matter how large or powerful, can entirely control its own destiny.

With these caveats in mind, let me enter into the topic in a more positive spirit. I will suggest four areas for universities throughout the world to attend to as they attempt to influence for the good their respective cultures.

First, reflect for a moment on the tripartite scheme of analysis quite commonly employed to evaluate present and future forms of cultural development—namely, *gender, race* and *class*. Such categories emerged from the world of high culture, that is, from the university and from learned commentators on contemporary life, particularly in the post-Enlightenment period of Western culture. In an effort to provoke a change in consciousness and a resulting abandonment of alienating and oppressive cultural structures, these thinkers have spoken out on behalf of the so-called "underclass," that is, those who are marginalized and suffer within the present system. There is a certain irony here, since often the few speak on behalf of the many without any effort at consultation. One must wonder whether such viewpoints do not lend themselves to demagoguery and excessively conflictive attitudes about social progress.

Nevertheless, at least in Western societies (and I suspect to a growing extent elsewhere), gender, race, and class will continue to provide an approach to culture that is both *descriptive* and *prescriptive*. More and more individuals will reflect on their experience as women and men, members of racial and ethnic groups, and participants in various economic structures and, on the basis of perceived inequities, will advocate cultural structures that assume human respect, just treatment, and a proper degree of political participation.

Universities need to welcome the opportunity to contribute to this process of cultural analysis, a process that should begin in the very structuring of university life itself. In the United States, for example, determined efforts are under way to assure a more multicultural and international environment on our campuses. This requires (a) active recruitment of and financial support for a more diversified faculty and student body, (b) the promotion of internal support systems for those who, perhaps for the first time, experience themselves as "minorities," and (c) a review of the curriculum so that it encompasses a broader frame of historical and cultural reference both in content and interconnectedness.

In many ways, the most crucial role that universities can play, relative to the volatile issues of gender, race, and class, is to remain open forums where a range of opinions and judgments can be entertained and freely discussed without fear of censure, violence, or arrest. Academic freedom is not first of all about professorial prerogatives but about the power of ideas to change and transform. Academic freedom springs from the conviction that the truth, and only the truth, can lead to genuine human progress.

This first point—the significance of the categories of gender, race, and class—leads to a second one. True learning takes place not only in the exposure to theoretical categories of cultural analysis in the classroom, in the laboratory, or before the computer screen, but also through *experiential education.* This is the second area universities must attend to. Experiential education is that series of activities that encourage the student or faculty member to enter into and learn from the life experiences of people different from themselves. One result of this type of sustained exposure can be an enhanced sense of cultural sensitivity and a greater appreciation for the richness of cultural diversity.

Experiential education encompasses a wide range of potential activities. At a minimum it requires a planned variation from the accustomed routines of academic life. One way to structure new learning opportunities is to focus on service. In the United States, for example, there are several national movements (Campus Compact, COOL, YES) to encourage students at every level of education to become involved in their local communities in order to assist the elderly, the young, the addicted, and other people in need. These projects are compatible timewise with the students' formal academic responsibilities. From their own testimony, students usually return from such endeavors with a fuller realization of the reality of poverty or aging or racial/ethnic prejudice and with a new set of questions for their professors. There are no guarantees that service projects will significantly impact the learning process, but the evidence seems overwhelming that this is the case.

A second way that experiential education can take place is through foreign studies programs. In the United States, languages are often studied but seldom mastered to the point of fluency. Fortunately, this is beginning to change. By integrating the study in the classroom of grammar, literature, and culture with concrete immersion in foreign cultural settings, students can be more properly motivated. What was once an obstacle course on the way to graduation becomes the source of future options for work and further study.

A third way to achieve experiential education is through various on-site work and apprenticeship programs. The pre-professional student who volunteers in the hospital or clinic, the budding young lawyer who reviews legal briefs in an office, the student of architecture who interns with an architectural firm, and the accounting student who helps prepare tax returns are all testing what they have learned in class and entering into the practice of a possible future profession. This interplay between theory and practice is crucial for preparing thoughtful and creative leaders for the future.

I have listed at least three ways that experiential education can take place under university auspices—through projects of voluntary service, through foreign studies programs, and through internship programs in the workplace. There are surely others. The important point is that our comprehension of culture in the fullest sense is affected decisively both by our theoretical appraisal of what forces underlie its structures and by our capacity to move outside the comfortable and familiar points of normal access to culture toward a view which can include the life experience of people different from ourselves.

The third area to consider is the role and place of the fine and performing arts in our universities and the general influence of the media in our respective cultures. This is the age of instant communications. Tastes in music, styles of fashion, a pervasive youth culture, and vicarious participation in dramatic events taking place in other nations have all been made possible by the ubiquity of radio, television, and movies. The influence of the media reaches even into the most impoverished and isolated settings. Collectively, we watch students dance on the Berlin Wall, protest in Tienanmen Square, and cavort on Florida's beaches. Some astute and domineering governments, wary of internal revolt or external pressures for reform, attempt to control the sources of news and suppress the artistic display of any but the most banal or apolitical material.

Universities have traditionally been centers for the study and development of the arts, including criticism. Theatre companies, musical groups, art galleries, museums, and campus radio and television stations have provided students firsthand opportunities to master the cultural heritage of the past and to make creative contributions to contemporary cultural life. In a literal sense, universities prepare the next generation to be a receptive audience for the best that the human spirit can devise.

There is perhaps no greater danger to any culture than that its creative arts atrophy from neglect or non-support and, as a result, produce only junk. It is an obligation of every center of learning that it teach students to discern the different degrees of quality and excellence available in the artifacts, compositions, and texts of the day. This is neither to defend entrenched cultural conservatism nor to baptize, as it were, the fads and fashions of the moment. While no human canon need be given sacred status, substance and style are goods in their own right and some works of art seem to capture with a high level of skill the deepest yearnings of the human heart.

No human institution is as well situated as the university to be both a contributor to and a critic of the fine and performing arts. Consequently, from rock music to the World Cup, from *Rambo* to *Henry V*, the university has a special role to play in assessing the state and condition of the popular media and popular culture.

The fourth and final area I would suggest is the study of religion and its cultural impact. Since I am a Roman Catholic priest this may sound a bit self-serving. However, even the briefest reflection suggests that religion as a personal commitment continues to influence the behavior of millions of people and, even more, religious movements remain a powerful force for better or ill in our world. All of the predictions of the cultured despisers of religion and all of the cynicism fostered in a generally hostile academy (particularly in the West) have not been sufficient to eliminate the significance of the religious dimension of reality.

What is the continuing appeal of Judaism, Christianity, and Islam in a post-secularist society? Will Buddhism, Hinduism, Shintoism, Confucianism, or other primarily Eastern manifestations of religion survive persecution by Communist regimes or the general acceptance of scientific methodology and a scientific world view? Are pilgrimages, devotional practices, and sacred art a recrudescence of ancient (and therefore primitive) sensibilities? Much is being written today about religious fundamentalism and its cultural impact. Few personalities generate the media attention of Pope John Paul II or the Dalai Lama. The breakup of modern empires is a reminder of how religious and/or ethnic loyalties and hatred can survive even long periods of quiescence.

Religion is worthy of study because it is an integral part of the cultural history of the human species. Even today, adherents of various religious traditions interpret reality through their theological prisms. From these standpoints they contribute to the common culture in all of its manifestations. They produce art and censor it as well. They propose political courses of action and critique those they find hostile. They sometimes suffer persecution for their beliefs and other times inflict it. A university that dismisses this whole complex weave as mere superstition or a childish residue of immature consciousness renders itself incapable of addressing the full range of human values and conduct.

Some Guidelines for
Social Justice Education

Some time ago, a futurologist writing in *The Christian Science Monitor* listed six great issues facing humanity at the turn of the millennium. He had compiled the list based on interviews with leading personalities in the United States and abroad. The first great issue—and the most prominent—was the dilemma of nuclear war, because it calls into question the very survival of the species. The next four issues were somewhat predictable—for example, the relationship between the First and the Third Worlds. But the last one was the most curious. This group of national and international leaders felt that one of the most troubling issues to be faced in the 1990s and beyond was the breakdown of public and private morality. Their fear was that we could not even begin to address some of the other pressing issues unless we first could agree on common values with which to build public consensus. These commentators felt that we desperately needed an operative framework within which we could address basic questions like the nature of a healthy family, the role of women, ecological sensitivity, world hunger, and other planetary crises.

Higher education can contribute to the solution of these problems in a number of ways, including the research carried on at our institutions and the open forum we provide for discussion and debate on the crucial issues. Our principal contribution, however, is our preparation of students—in the classroom and beyond—to be both able and willing to tackle these issues.

The education that comes from beyond the classroom is my focus here. In particular, I focus on the idea of experiential education, the university as the setting for this kind of education, and some related theses of my own.

Experiential Education

I do not know, of course, how particular individuals first become involved in matters of ethics, of social justice, and of peace. I suppose all of us have our own stories, anecdotes that we can tell about our past, about our upbringing, about the encounters that we had in our neighborhoods and in our education and afterwards. All I know is that some people are more acutely aware than others of questions of social justice. Trying to account for that and, more importantly, trying to stimulate awareness in the next generation is, I think, a central element of our collective mission.

I grew up in Washington, D.C., where I was exposed to the whole question of race and its significance. I observed in the District a certain measure of the poverty that exists in any major urban setting. And I came from a family that took religious values seriously—when major issues were debated in the newspapers or on television and radio, my sisters and I had only to ask to learn what our parents' opinions were. As a family, we were urban Catholics in a city with a majority black population.

My first two years as an undergraduate at Notre Dame were relatively uneventful. However, one day during my junior year I overheard a conversation in the hall concerning a group of students who were going to Mexico. Because I was a scholarship athlete, I had a certain amount of economic flexibility in the summer, and this allowed me to consider being part of the project myself. The idea came completely "out of the blue." All I can say is that I happened to hear a conversation and my curiosity was aroused. As it turned out, however, that summer venture was for me the opening of a whole new world. What I learned during that and subsequent trips to Peru and Mexico I took back to the classrooms of Notre Dame, asking questions that were radically different from those I was accustomed to asking. I began to have a real awareness of inequality, of inequitable distribution of wealth, of cultural discrimination, and of many other conditions I had read about in books and heard about in lectures, but which until then had not sunk in in quite the same way. A liveliness and an intense curiosity toward the educational opportunities available to me in the university setting flowed naturally from the experiences that I had in the summer.

Twenty years later, I was provided another opportunity to broaden my perspective of justice and peace matters when I participated in a two-week Maryknoll program for university educators. In some ways this program replicated what I had been through as a student. However, now I was older and more experienced and had a professional identity as a priest and educator. I brought back a different kind of vision. Now the relevant question was what could I do as a teacher to communicate this intellectual experience in ways appropriate to the classroom and the pulpit.

Finally, several years ago under the auspices of the Association of Catholic Colleges and Universities, I went to Costa Rica to explore what the relationship might be between the United Nations' University of Peace and various Catholic institutions. This time it was not so much a coming to grips with the reality of poverty, but rather exploring a related question—Was there an intercultural context in which the question of peace could be explored more effectively than just within national boundaries?

On the basis of these personal encounters over some twenty-five years, I see two kinds of experiential education—

one a brief immersion and the other a sustained, long-term commitment. Both have a place in education, for often the second flows out of the first.

An example of the brief immersion is a program called the Urban Plunge. It is a 48-hour exposure to a side of American life with which most university students are not personally acquainted. It has the following qualities: It is *raw*, i.e., it is a disjunctive situation; it does not conform to what the typical student has known firsthand before. It is *concentrated*: Students see a great deal more than they can absorb. And it is *personally unprecedented*. Part of the impact is that the students have not had that kind of opportunity before. The rawness, I think, makes a huge difference. If you are going to structure something to jog or stimulate someone's consciousness, it has got to be poignant enough to be different from what people are accustomed to.

Another feature of the brief immersion is that it must be *structured*. If a program is going to make maximum use of little time, students cannot spend it in cars or buses or walking around with no sense of what they are seeing. Also crucial is the question of who supervises the experience. People who work day after day in these same settings are the best guides. In fact, one of the major problems we face as a national school with Urban Plunges set up in more than 60 sites around the country is ensuring that there are enough willing and qualified supervisors.

A crucial component of the brief immersion is what happens when the students return to campus. To reinforce their experiences, students should be asked to write about them and also should be given the opportunity to compare notes with fellow students who have had similar experiences.

Whether one calls it an Urban Plunge or a Rural Plunge or an Appalachian Experience, there is great value to these brief immersions—and because of the modest demand on students' time, these programs offer fewer excuses for not participating. Our experience at Notre Dame suggests that this seemingly minimal activity often is the beginning of a real commitment by students to assume a substantial, long-term role in the pursuit of social justice.

This second stage of experiential learning has its own necessary elements. The first is *meaningful work* sustained long enough (here is the importance of summers) that one can become part of the rhythm of life of a people and place, can allow the sights, the smells, and the sounds to get into the soul, in a sense. Even now, for example, I can vividly recall some of the places that I have been in Peru and Chile and Mexico and still can almost smell the garbage dumps that one walks by, the sewage, the dust in the air. I can see the bloated stomachs and the dilapidated housing and all the consequences of the lack of water. The unemployed sitting around, the neighborhood drunks making a scene at night keeping everybody awake, the dogs yapping, the cats yowling—whether in this country or abroad, becoming part of the rhythm of life is essential to having a real experience of poverty.

Time for discussion and reflection, both with experts and with the local people, is readily available in these longer-range projects and can help reveal the underside of things. For example, I am an "urban freak." I like to give tours of cities. On occasion, I have taken people to a street corner in a major city and said, "I would like you to stand here for forty-five minutes, and then I would like you to tell me what you see. Then we'll talk about it, and I'll tell you what I see, since I may have a little more experience and background." The same can be done on a trip to an urban park to watch the dynamics, or by having people explore the same setting in the morning, at lunchtime, at dinnertime, and at night. All of this is to get people to begin to appreciate the different worlds of the same site, to give them new perspectives on what is really going on. The panhandlers, pickpockets, sexual overtures, drugs—all are there, but people often cannot see them for these things blend into the background of urban life.

The final component of the semester or summer project is debriefing. What happens when people return from long-range projects? Who engages them in conversation and reflection? What do they read? If they have kept a diary or a journal, who helps them sort out their experiences? This is the essential component that universities and colleges can provide to make experiential learning a pedagogically sound experience. Once students have had these opportunities, what they bring to the books and to the classroom or into the laboratories is considerably enhanced.

The University Setting

From my vantage point—as a person who has been a teacher and lived in a dorm (and still does) and now is an administrator entrusted with responsibility for the institution as a whole, including social justice and peace education— at this particular moment of American Catholic history, the question of institutional self-definition is critical. Institutional survival and well-being are a direct function of our preservation of a meaningful self-definition. What does it mean to be a Catholic college or university? We all know that debate; it goes on endlessly. (I am always amused to hear people not in Catholic education asking each other what it means to be a secular institution. Anyway, we are not the only people who go through this.)

Institutional self-definition—for us, what it means to be a Catholic school—encompasses, I think, these requirements: serious regard for the range of courses students take (including, for many institutions, requirements in philosophy and theology); the provision of opportunities for worship; concern for pastoral care; and (and I stress the equal importance of this) the inculcation of a commitment to social responsibility as citizens and as members of the church. Because this last objective can only be accomplished if students have come to grips in some organized way with the major issues of the day, social justice education is crucial and necessary for Catholic colleges and universities.

Administrators need to make certain to integrate social justice education into institutional priorities. This means structuring the common life to provide maximum opportunities for students and others to grapple in some organized way with the great issues. It means looking closely at both our sources and uses of funds. If social justice is used as a goad to interest people in the university and the money raised is spent for other purposes, then our actions obviously are inconsistent with our stated mission.

Administrators must serve as models—inside and outside the university community. What the president and the provost do, what the deans and other administrators do with their time—the issues and the programs they are interested in—all of this makes a significant difference in how people view the university. At Notre Dame, we have organized an Urban Plunge for administrators and local community leaders. Fifteen of us participated in a recent one. We went to about twelve agencies— the welfare department, the county jail, the state prison. We visited alternate treatment programs for prisoners. We went to the county prosecutor's office and to an institution that takes care of the physically and mentally handicapped. We stopped at a house where students and ex-cons live together and try to form a community. We did all of this with the president of a local bank, with two corporate CEOs, with a local politician, and others from the university. It was a very healthy interaction, one that established a momentum for the years ahead.

Faculty involvement with and support of justice and peace education is essential to the full integration of these subjects into the academic life of the university. Curriculum structuring is the first hurdle to overcome. Some years ago during his presidency of Notre Dame, Father Hesburgh attempted to establish a values seminar for seniors. Arts and Letters people nodded, "Wonderful idea"; most of the rest of the faculty sighed, "Who's going to teach this material?" Beset by faculty fears of stepping outside their areas of professional training and by faculty indifference, the seminar never got off the ground. Since then, proposals have been made to require all students to investigate social justice issues either through an experiential learning project or through particular courses, but the closest we have come to that has been an improvement of our course offerings combined with many extracurricular activities.

Why are such proposals for a curricular base for social justice issues resisted by the faculty? Partly, I think, the reluctance stems from the absence of a preparatory graduate school specialization, partly it reflects our habit of passing along responsibility for social justice education, and partly it reveals a real fear on the part of people that if they are forced to do this, they are going to be so noticeably incompetent that their careers will be somehow damaged. There also are people, of course, who are just totally uninterested in social justice. We have to admit that. But the larger problem has more to do with specialization and fear than with lack of interest.

A second faculty concern is whether justice and peace education is soft or hard reflection. Is there room, they ask, for analysis and criticism or will it be just a recitation of soft-hearted and idealistic progressivism? Answering this question makes it evident that scholarly consideration of social justice must engage the very best minds, and that faculty who teach in this area full time must be respected among their peers as teachers and scholars who can hold their own with anyone. Quality is essential.

That said, the question of hard or soft reflection still is not an easy one to sort out, much like the question of quantitative versus qualitative analysis in economics or political science. Is all knowledge distilled in computer programs or are the real questions about social values unearthed in the research and writing we do? My instinct as an ethicist is always to beware the temptation of the "quick fix" and to see complexity, rather than simplicity. For any issue or problem, I usually can identify twenty-five variables that must be taken into account and perhaps seven alternative courses of action.

That is the way I have been trained, the way I think, and when someone steps up to tell me there is only one way to see a particular issue and only one course to follow, my every instinct bristles and says, "That's just not true." Part of what people mean by the distinction between hard and soft analysis is the recognition that reality is much more diverse and complex than simple schemes of amelioration can encompass.

The third area of faculty involvement in social justice education is ethics. We must continue to push across the boundaries, not to allow faculty to relegate all consideration of ethics to the College of Arts and Letters. The inclination to consider these issues generally is stronger in the humanities, the social sciences, and the fine arts and may not be so prevalent elsewhere in the university.

Ethics actually is a growth business right now. The need for intense study of problems and principles has spawned a number of impressive think tanks including the Hastings Institute, which focuses on biomedical ethics, and the Kennedy Institute at Georgetown. The topics taken up by these and other centers have ranged from war and peace to business ethics.

Of late, all of the major professions have been subject to intense ethical scrutiny. When a prominent denizen of Wall Street gives $20 million to the Harvard Business School to solve the profession's problems, that would appear to signal a general malaise. In law, medicine, government service, education, the ministry, in fact throughout the so-called classic professions, there are symptoms of failure—not in terms of the rigor of preparation, or the difficulty of entry, or the existence and communication of codes of ethics, but in terms of adherence to and enforcement of those codes by members of the professions. This is the persistent dilemma of professional life in our time, and its solution must involve educational institutions.

But what of students? How can they be motivated to become interested and involved in social justice education?

I have suggested experiential education as the first step. But what will prompt them to volunteer in the first place? It is not enough to trust to chance—to imagine that they, as I did, will overhear someone talking down the hall when they happen to have a summer free and adequate financial support to permit them to participate. First, we have to be better at public relations. The leaders among our students must be identified and cultivated, which means confronting head-on the premature professionalization of our students and their prepackaged career paths, i.e. "I'm pre-med; I don't have any time for that stuff" or "Engineering takes every hour that I have." One approach is to give increased prominence and visibility to students who already have participated in social service projects and can be effective spokespersons among their peers.

Another fact to be met head-on is the financial need of many individuals. For example, students who otherwise would eagerly participate in a summer service project may simply not be able to forego the income from a summer job. At Notre Dame, a program underwritten by our alumni clubs and by the James F. Andrews Scholarship Fund addresses this problem by providing Social Concerns Tuition Scholarships of $1,400 to eligible students who spend eight weeks as part of a project assisting the poor in an alumni club city. Aside from helping with students' financial problems, this program provides all the other benefits of interaction I mentioned earlier. Before, during, and after the experience, the students have regular opportunities to discuss social concerns with the members of the sponsoring alumni club, with the social service professionals involved in the programs, and with the people being assisted. So successful has this program been that Yale and Stanford now are establishing their own programs based on ours.

One concern at Notre Dame, which I suspect also applies to other schools, is how to increase participation in these programs by men, who—at least proportionately—are far less likely than women to become involved. One of the healthy characteristics of the American Catholic Church, compared with the church in Europe, has been the widespread involvement of men in every facet of church life, including voluntary associations. That participation, however, is wanting when it comes to male student involvement in social justice matters. It is a situation that needs to be publicly aired and addressed.

Minority student participation in social justice work also lags. Many who have lived or live close to the raw experience in their own lives are reluctant to revisit such situations. They are striving to be part of the success story, the elite who have broken out. To be too quickly thrust back into an all too familiar situation can be a very frightening and unpleasant experience. Ironically, then, those students with the most relevant personal experiences do not want to relive them, although if they would, they could be great interpreters and bridge builders.

Some Theses

By way of conclusion, I offer the following assorted theses —all apropos to education for justice and peace.

Experience enlivens consciousness. This is not a new nor a dramatic claim. Experience cannot, however, always be firsthand. The direct, immediate experience of poverty or violence or conflict is only one vehicle for involving people in matters of justice and peace. There is also the way of the imagination, of symbol, of story. In my personal reading on questions of war and peace, for example, Walter Miller's novel, *A Canticle for Lebowitz*, moved me intensely. Similarly, in Stanley Kubrick's film *Barry Lyndon* there is a striking image of the insanity of war—troops marching across a field into intense cannon fire, never ducking but marching upright in classic nineteenth-century military style. The same film examines the irony of dueling with its code of honor and rubrical niceties. Novels and films such as these, as well as thematic art, certainly enhance our ability to engage in sophisticated and subtle discussion about war and its alternatives.

Universities and colleges are particularly well suited to promote this artistic stimulation. Readings, film series, and art displays ought, to be an integral part of our efforts to enliven the consciousness of our communities.

Reality is complex, and progress toward justice and peace is usually slow and difficult. If one is fully reflective, reads the literature, and works with the people in the front lines, it is easy to become discouraged and lose hope. That is why it is so difficult to sustain people's interest in these issues. To recognize signs of progress, to celebrate even minor victories, is crucial to the process of developing a lifetime commitment to social justice and peace.

The worst alternative is to lose hope. We need stories of success. We need heroic figures. We need to repeat again and again the stories of individuals like Martin Luther King, Jr., Dorothy Day, and others of their calibre who persisted in protest against injustice, even sacrificing their lives. On the other hand, how many individuals have taken on an impressive agenda of service activities only to be emotionally overwhelmed in the process, either from lack of support or because their understanding of the burden they had assumed was too naive. The worst alternative is to lose hope.

Colleges and universities as institutions are better at analysis than at advocacy. This is perhaps a controversial theory, but, I believe, accurate. Colleges and universities are best suited to dissect problems, describe their components, and organize alternatives. There is always pressure on institutions, however, to advocate movements, causes, or prophetic stances. When institutions and their leadership refuse to become formal advocates of various causes, accusations of weak will and lack of courage inevitably follow. My response is that the way we structure ourselves is in itself a kind of advocacy, but with regard to advocating a particular cause, I continue to counsel great caution. Advocacy is best left to the various concerned organizations that flourish within the university or college community.

Colleges and universities are and should be places where the church does its thinking. Father Ted Hesburgh insisted on this point throughout his career, and I wholeheartedly agree. One of the great achievements in Catholic history is the system of higher education in this country. Not to appreciate the success and the influence that our institutions have had on the well-being of the church as well as the nation is, I think, very short-sighted. The church indeed does its thinking in our institutions. Our institutional self-definition, our mission, our role, is indispensable to the church as a community of thinking and discourse as well as of service.

Campus Policing Symposium Keynote Address

As the issues surrounding crime and crime prevention have come to the fore in recent years, the question has been raised, To what extent ought we to professionalize law enforcement? That is, to what extent does law enforcement resemble the learned professions as not just a job, but a way of life requiring a particular preparation over and above basic skills? Because campus policing has reached an advanced maturity, these questions, it seems to me, apply to campus as well as civil law enforcement.

In general terms, professionalization involves specialized training, the mastering of a formalized system of knowledge that is not commonly learned. Examples in law enforcement would include gaining the expertise to carry a weapon and earning the authority to make arrests. But professionalization also requires a code, a set of principles and practices to which every practitioner is held accountable and which is enforced by other members of the profession.

Over the years, law enforcement has had codes of a kind, and people have been held accountable to these codes. But my suspicion is that, at least in this country, oftentimes the code of law enforcement has been insufficiently articulated, training has been rudimentary, and expectations—particularly of private security services—have not been high.

What I think is happening at colleges and universities across the country today is that problems are growing more severe, therefore the level of expectation for security is rising, therefore there is a greater demand for professionalization.

Professionalization in law enforcement often has focused on the question of education, i.e., what level of training—high school, college, police academy—is necessary for what level of responsibility. In civil law enforcement the presumption generally has been that the greater the level of responsibility, the higher the level of training necessary. I am not sure that that always has been the case in campus law enforcement, but it is interesting to note that chief law enforcement officers on campuses typically have been drawn from outside, that is, from municipal, state, military and other police agencies whose educational and training requirements typically have been more stringent than those for campus police.

I would argue strongly in favor of increased professionalization of law enforcement, in general and on campus, and along with that I would agree both that financial rewards should rise with the level of skill required and that significantly greater leadership training ought to be required of those in administrative authority. Both of these issues constitute major problems in many campus police forces today.

We all know miscreants and incompetents in our professions. I can say, as an academic administrator, a university faculty member, and a member of the ministry, that I know people in all three professions who do what they do poorly, because of illness, addiction, self-aggrandizement, or because they are outright frauds. Some such cases become public knowledge and scandals result, but we all know that every profession has its own instinct of self-preservation. We fear that if we hold members of our professions publicly accountable for their misdeeds, such cases will to a degree discredit all of us. The sad fact, of course, is that the ultimate result of, not holding people accountable is even greater scandal and even greater loss of credibility, trust, and respect.

Against this overall background, what are some of the issues that we face in campus law enforcement? The most mundane yet most persistent and frustrating problem of all is parking. I would be willing to wager that this is the number one headache because, on most campuses, there simply is not enough space for everyone to park as close as they would like to where they work or live. Perhaps the situation is most severe in urban surroundings where parking is a problem on and off campus. We like to think of our campus as a community in the best sense of the term and we like to put our best foot forward at all times. Nobody wants to give tickets or refuse access, yet we know that, for the best functioning of the institution, both steps are necessary. I mention this business of parking first, because it seems the furthest removed from violence and because it is a headache that is always with us. But the fact also is that "parking police" is the dominant image many people have of campus law enforcement.

"If my car is parked five minutes too long, they're writing a ticket, but they're never there when you really need them" is an often heard complaint on college campuses. Another is "They're never there when a crime is committed because they're too busy towing cars."

This image of campus security is ample evidence of the need for professionalization, the need for campus officers whose demeanor is testimony to their training and competence and whose performance demonstrates a mastery of police techniques.

The challenge all of us face is to make it possible for campuses to remain communities of scholars where interaction is abundant and productive, personal and wholesome, and safe and secure—and, at the same time, to preserve campuses as places where the broadest possible range of public expression, public demonstration and public protest is tolerated even as the business of learning is protected from unwarranted interference. That is a tall order.

Virtually every educational institution in the country is becoming a progressively more racially, more ethnically diverse community, and at some times in some places this evolution has been and will be a source of tensions. No one can be solely blamed for misunderstandings that are rooted deep in our backgrounds and in the history of our nation. But blame is sometimes assessed for every trait down to the style of music people enjoy or the way they party. Nothing is more potentially volatile in these situations than the role and conduct of campus police. They, on behalf of all of us, are asked to intervene when people find themselves affronted by what other members of the community say or do.

As the result of past incidents on campuses across the country, we all are much more aware of the things that grate and of what we must do to avoid inflicting hurt and disrespect. And it seems to me that, in their work, campus police deserve, from administrators and faculty and students and staff, recognition that often they are asked to do the hard thing, to intervene and to assess the causes of something that may have no obvious cause at all aside from a broad cultural cause.

The campus police must be prepared for this role, unpleasant and unpopular as it might be. Indeed, there is no area of sensitivity training more important than that dealing with the facts of race and ethnicity. We are trying to do something in this country that no other part of the world has ever accomplished very well, that in fact few societies have even attempted—to bring together in an environment of higher education people from widely varying backgrounds. And we are experiencing some degree of failure in this attempt. But it is an undertaking that is right, that deserves a commitment from us all, and that calls for a very sophisticated response from our law enforcement agencies.

Campus Policing Symposium Keynote Address

A second, related issue has to do with gender and the growing recognition that on university campuses, criminal acts too often have gone unreported because of the victims' fear of further humiliation by the community-at-large. Law enforcement is not responsible for that. Changing the culture of disrespect for women is first an educational and then a law enforcement challenge. Virtually every campus in the nation is developing new policies addressing relationships not only between students, but also between faculty and students and staff members and students.

How can we do a better job dealing with sexual misconduct when Americans generally accept high levels of sexual activity among the young as neither unexpected nor abnormal? If greater freedom of sexual expression is condoned among those the ages of our students, and if some percentage of these students have been led, even encouraged, to think that "no" does not necessarily mean "no," and especially when alcohol and/or drugs are introduced into the equation, then a situation has been created that is bound to result in abuses. Perhaps this situation is nothing new to the human race, but perhaps also the contemporary attitude toward sexuality contributes to a greater incidence of abuse than in the past.

In just the past year I (and every college or university president I know could tell a similar story) have had to look at these incidents from all perspectives. Women students come forward, sometimes days or weeks after an incident and only after the intervention of others. In response, student affairs personnel try to use their normal judicial procedures and, typically, receive mixed testimony from friends, or friends of friends, of those allegedly involved. Protection of victims, as well as of the rights of accused, is a critical part of the process. So is maintaining confidentiality, while at the same time attempting to reassure the community that no false sense of security is being created and that no proven act of misconduct is going unpunished. But because of the nature

– 135 –

of such cases, the punishment in the end may pale by comparison to civil penalties, and then the recriminations can begin: wails of protest from the offending student's family, even from friends and parents of friends, all protesting unfairness and claiming that the University is responsible for what has occurred. And all the time we know that in the case at hand the victim could have taken her charges to the courts, but chose not to because she did not want to get the offender "in that much trouble."

This sort of story is appearing in the media more and more regularly today, and many parents very legitimately are pressuring universities to be more aggressive in educating students on this issue. At the same time, they expect us to be more adept in handling our internal judicial processes, so that the innocent are protected yet a clear and consistent message is sent that some conduct is utterly and in every instance unacceptable.

Always, of course, we are part of a process that regards the accused as innocent until proven guilty, no matter how difficult proof is to obtain in these cases, no matter that we know there are many sexual crimes committed by nice-looking people who, in a hearing, appear to be the most innocent people in the world or who glibly assert that what happened was "ok" or that "we were both drunk" or that "fifty other people did it without getting into trouble, so what's different about me?"

I feel the pressure of these crimes, as every university administrator ought to. Our campus law enforcement officers are caught in the middle. Even though they are trying to do their job and create a climate of safety and security for men and women, when something goes wrong, their procedures must be sensitive enough to provide comfort and support to the victim, but also aggressive enough to apprehend the offenders.

Sexual misconduct, especially acquaintance rape, is the most difficult security and police issue we have to deal with, and the increased attention being given to campus and community crime statistics is going to ensure that this issue remains at the forefront of campus discussion and debate.

A third serious issue is the use of alcohol and drugs. I have served over several years as a member both of Governor Evan Bayh's Commission for a Drug-Free Indiana and President Bush's Advisory Council on Drugs. I have listened to law enforcement agents, to educators, to therapists, and to community leaders from all across the country. In some ways, I think we are making progress. Beginning in preschool, there is a growing recognition of the destructiveness of drugs, and this recognition is making its way onto our campuses. More people are coming to acknowledge the harm and the addictive pull of even those drugs once regarded on college campuses as an expression of the bohemian life or as a means of demonstrating freedom to experiment with life. We have begun to learn the lessons that emerge from all the tragedies.

But in the midst of this seeming success, alcohol continues to be the most tragic drug of choice of the high school and college population. Alcohol tends to be a very difficult thing to deal with, particularly when campus police have been soured by notions that college students are spoiled brats whose families typically bail them out of trouble and who will be abusive when they are drunk, yet look completely innocent when they are sober.

The whole notion of alcohol for those under twenty-one as "acceptable (in such-and-such a place under such-and-such conditions) but unacceptable (in civil law)" creates a true dilemma for most campus police forces. We address violations of drug statutes unambiguously, but not so alcohol. In an era when the so-called "drinking age" is universally twenty-one, we should be able to do a better, more consistent job of addressing illegal alcohol use.

Federal law requires every college and university that receives federal funding to state in print what its drug policy is. Increasingly, these policies involve drug testing, including of those involved in law enforcement. Such testing can be done cleanly, clearly, and fairly, and I think it can create greater confidence in and support for police as the campus enforcers of anti-drug statutes and rules.

These issues have for the most part involved the campus community itself. What about the relationship of the campus to the larger, surrounding community—and about the community's impact on campus? A great many American college and university campuses are situated in or near deteriorating urban neighborhoods, and it is becoming increasingly difficult to discharge our responsibilities toward our students when a number of them live or congregate where we have no direct authority.

The reputation of universities in a highly competitive student recruiting environment is going to be at least partially determined by whether they are seen as safe or unsafe. For this reason, if for none better, it is in everyone's best interest that universities become actively engaged in issues of the quality of life of contiguous neighborhoods.

At the most basic level, good "town-gown" relations begin with good relationships between campus police and their city, county, or state counterparts and between the administration and the mayor, governor, county executives or other local government executives.

The neighborhood around us is a varied community, including a number of our students. On pleasant weekends in the fall and spring, some among these students become neighborhood nuisances—loud, drunk, and disorderly. Some of these same students fail to keep up the properties they rent, driving down property values over time. We also have some slum lords who rent to students and who themselves do not maintain their properties, so the students at times cannot be blamed for living as they do in the environment to which they are subjected.

We have tried to address all the problems, real and potential, in this situation, by meeting regularly with the neighborhood organizations (in fact, a University staff member is vice president of one organization) and with the housing authority, the police and fire departments, the neighborhood planners and the people involved in economic development. We have tried to bring all these groups together so they know each other and communicate with each other and so are able at least to avoid those situations that develop when people at a distance from one another each blame their problems on the other.

More recently, we have faced problems of serious deterioration and the introduction of the drug trade in the local neighborhood. These developments, of course, pose a serious threat both to the future of the neighborhood and to the safety of its residents, including our students. What is more, large numbers of our students who do not live in the neighborhood do frequent the student "hangouts" located there and even more regularly pass through the area on the way to and from campus.

We have moved aggressively to address this new threat to the community. Along with city government and the leadership of a large medical center in the neighborhood, we have met with our counterparts on other campuses in other communities—the University of Chicago, for example—to see what steps they have taken in similar circumstances. The three of us now have agreed to fund a full-scale urban study by an outside consultant to determine concrete steps to be taken to arrest the deterioration of the neighborhood before the stability of the community is destroyed and the incidence of crime multiplies even further.

Our need to respond as institutions to these very complex and sensitive urban problems argues again for increased professionalization of campus police. First, if we are to keep our campuses under our own control, then our police must be fully capable of investigating, analyzing and, to the degree possible, preventing the wide array of "street crimes"—burglary, larceny, etc.—that are more frequently affecting campus life. Second, to cooperate at peak efficiency with local law enforcement agencies, campus police must be regarded by those other agencies as competent fellow professionals, capable of engaging in any police activity.

What does the president of a university expect of his or her campus security and police? I begin by expecting that our goal of keeping the campus a true community will be advanced by every segment of that community. To that end, I believe campus police must clearly recognize both what their responsibilities are and where they end. They must give top priority at all times to maintaining clear lines of communication both up the line to their superiors and along the lines to the community-at-large and in all normal circumstances create a positive, welcoming environment on campus. They must take pains, as indeed we all should, to be servants of the community, to be prepared to act swiftly and decisively in those unwanted situations where confrontation is necessary to protect the community, and in general, to have the knowledge to design and implement the most effective, yet least intrusive policies for protecting the community's ability to function and its overall quality of life.

What I—what we all—reject is the spectre of a campus where all feel like strangers, where the night is feared, where much time is spent looking over shoulders, where some members of the community encounter a prevailing suspicion and disrespect, where good will is lost in recrimination and placing blame, and where victims fear to speak or come forward.

I believe that by applying professional standards to our campus police, by hiring good people and paying equitable salaries and seeing to it that our personnel are representative of the entire university population, we can, in fact, avoid that nightmare and achieve the community we desire.

And I would suggest that there is no time like the present to pursue this goal.

Statement on Athletics

Notre Dame has a proud and long-established tradition of participation in intercollegiate athletics. Today, we face a new world with its own set of challenges and opportunities. It seems appropriate that I articulate as clearly as I can the central values and expectations, as well as the supporting structures, that will guide our institutional participation in intercollegiate athletics in the coming years.

For any of these tasks to be engaged in successfully, a certain level of ability and preparation is required. Even for those well suited by training and endowment the adjustment to the rigors of academic life in a highly competitive university setting may be difficult.

Basic Principles:

(i) No student athlete will be accepted into the University who does not possess, on the basis of the best available testing instruments, the capacity to complete successfully a baccalaureate degree at Notre Dame.

(ii) As part of a highly residential university where the majority of students live on-campus, student athletes will normally live in dormitories. However, there will be *no* separate dormitories or sections of dormitories restricted to student athletes. The goal is to have a complete integration of student athletes into the student body.

(iii) Because of the manifest harm connected to drug use in our society, particular attention will be given to providing education and counsel for all students and student athletes with regard to this matter. Whenever circumstances warrant it, there will also be random, unannounced drug testing for student athletes. The results of these tests will be dealt with according to a previously established policy made known to all student athletes.

(iv) Chaplains will regularly be provided for our athletic teams. Their duties will include pastoral care and liturgical service for athletes and coaches.

Coaching Staffs

Coaches are primarily teachers. They share with members of the faculty the responsibility to educate and train the students entrusted to them. Pedagogical methods and level of supervision will vary from sport-to-sport and according to rank. The University community should accord coaches the respect they deserve as co-sharers in the overall educational mission.

(i) The Executive Vice-President, in consultation with the Faculty Board and the Athletic Director, is responsible for the hiring of coaches. Normally, coaches will be hired for a specified period of time. The University expects to fulfill its responsibilities under these employments.

(ii) Coaches are expected to abide by the highest standards of personal conduct. They have the opportunity to influence the student athletes not only by the values they espouse but by their manner of life as well.

(iii) Coaches are expected to appreciate the importance attached to academic life in the Notre Dame experience and to express this appreciation in all activities associated with the recruitment, education, and participation of students in varsity and non-varsity athletics.

(iv) Coaches are held to the guidelines and rules agreed upon by the member institutions of the NCAA. This applies to recruitment, financial aid, team discipline, and other related matters. Any violation of these standards will be treated with utmost seriousness.

Athletic Administration

The Athletic Director and his staff are directly responsible for the administration of the athletic programs at Notre Dame. The Athletic Director reports to the Executive Vice-President.

(i) Notre Dame will endeavor to maintain a high-quality, competitive athletic program consistent with its heritage. If and when problems arise, public accountability will be given consistent with principles of justice and due process.

(ii) The total athletic program of the University will generate sufficient funds to be self-supporting. This should never be done to the detriment of the integrity of the institution or its identifiable priorities. There will be no booster clubs or other such entities outside of the direct control of the athletic department. The annual operating budget and the ongoing financial activities of the athletic department will be subject to the same review and approval process as are all other operating units of the University.

(iii) A full athletic program, consistent with the financial resources available and the overall academic program of the University, will be provided for men and women student athletes.

(iv) Coaches and athletic department personnel will, insofar as possible, reflect the racial, ethnic, and gender diversity of both the broader University community and society at large.

(v) Non-varsity athletics will be provided sufficient support to enable every student to have the opportunity to participate in some form of organized athletic activity.

Conclusion:

In sum, as an institution we will pursue a standard of achievement in athletics consistent with our overall purposes as a university. We will attempt to excel in every form of intercollegiate athletics, but not at the price of distorting our primary role as educators and moral guides. If we discover instances of misjudgment or abuse, we will strive speedily to rectify the situation.

We remain confident that Notre Dame and other institutions with similar values and goals can lead the way and shape a worthy standard for the special enterprise of intercollegiate athletics.

Aspiring to Greatness

*I*n its 150 years of existence, the University of Notre Dame has grown from a grade school parading as a university to an undergraduate college with a few advanced programs to its present status as a nationally renowned university with increasingly high aspirations in graduate education and research.

For more than a century the University developed in fits and starts depending on its leadership, faculty, and finances. To an extent unrecognized by many people, Notre Dame was the site of historic research breakthroughs beginning in the late nineteenth century. The first wireless transmission in the United States, pioneering demonstrations of the principles of flight, the discovery of synthetic rubber, the first successful bombardment of the nucleus of an atom, the development of germ-free animal populations and artificial environments all took place at the University, but all were achieved in the absence of any substantial underlying support structure. A medium-sized university with its four colleges and law school, Notre Dame entered the twentieth century significantly behind its current peer institutions. As late as 1952, when Father Hesburgh began his thirty-five years as president, Notre Dame suffered from an almost nonexistent endowment, poor budgetary procedures, and a dearth of affluent alumni and benefactors. Its growth in all these areas over the last forty years is one of the truly stunning success stories in American higher education.

What are the hallmarks of this success and how do we continue to advance in academic quality? The components of any fine university are the quality of its students at both the undergraduate and graduate levels; the strength of its faculty, including chaired professors; and the extent and quality of its library holdings, its classroom and research facilities, and its technology and support services.

Our undergraduate student body is among the most select in the nation, and even the recent decline in applications—a demographic phenomenon affecting all institution—has so far failed to dilute this quality. Our principal obstacle in attracting more of these students is the limit of our financial aid offerings. Because we refuse to use tuition dollars as a source of aid and because we insist that all financial awards be based strictly on students' need, we often lose qualified students who are offered large, merit-based scholarships by others. That is why our first priority now and for the foreseeable future is to increase our financial aid endowment. As a first step, we have committed to raise an additional $100 million in financial aid endowment by the year 2000, and our ultimate goal is to meet the full demonstrated need of every admitted student. We relish the pursuit of this goal, particularly at a time when some institutions are retreating from this commitment.

With regard to the quality of our graduate student body, we presently lag behind where we would like to be despite major advances in some departments such as theology, philosophy, physics, and chemical engineering. In these fields we are highly competitive. Our goal is not to become an institution like, for example, the University of Chicago, where fully two-thirds of the student body are graduate and professional students. "Small but superb" is the description we seek for our graduate school, and here, too, a significant improvement of our financial aid packages is the key. At the same time, we must do a better job of communicating the strength of our programs and faculty. On the positive side, our construction of new and attractive graduate student housing and our increased attention to the personal and social needs of graduate students should enhance our reputation.

We currently have more than seventy endowed professorships fully funded and occupied by distinguished faculty, with half again that number of chairs partially funded. This is a particularly telling indicator of our growth in distinction; just twenty years ago there was a total of four endowed professorships in the entire University.

Equally impressive has been the improvement of our academic facilities. The list of just those projects recently completed or at various stages of planning and construction includes a major addition to the Law School; a massive classroom facility able to seat half the student body at one time; a new College of Business building; an aerospace research center housing our wind tunnels, several of which are the only ones of their kind in the world; a major addition for advanced physics research in our College of Science; a performing arts center; a complete renovation of our School of Architecture; and building-by-building upgrading of all existing classroom and laboratory space on campus. At the same time, with one of the largest single dollar commitments in our history—more than $27 million—we have significantly expanded and enhanced our computer capabilities for instruction, research, and personal use by students and faculty.

Our library continues to suffer from a relatively low rating at the national level, partly due to the absence in the University of a medical or agricultural school. In the Hesburgh Library—popularly identified by its massive mural of Christ the teacher—we have one of the finest physical facilities in higher education, but our various branch libraries suffer from inadequate space. We have been incrementally adding to the library budget over the years and are making steady, although too slow progress. We are improving more in our purchases of new books and materials than we are in matching the staffing levels of our peer institutions' libraries. We are on the right track with the library, but we need additional resources to make faster progress.

As even this brief accounting of Notre Dame's physical and human resources suggests, our academic aspirations are ambitious, amounting to nothing less than excellence, and even more, to excellence that embodies our Catholic tradition, which holds that belief is the guide to inquiry. The university as an institution sprang from this concept, and we aim to be a university in the fullest sense.

Specifically, we want to achieve distinction at the graduate level equal to that which we have demonstrated in undergraduate education. We want to be more international in scope both in terms of curriculum and of the experience of other cultures available to our students. We want to identify the areas of current and potential strength in each of our colleges and departments so that we can put our resources to best use. We believe the era of being "all things to all people" in research has ended, and we do not propose to relive the experiences of universities that have become overcommitted and out of focus. We continue to evaluate our programs through internal and external reviews and have already combined, subdivided, or restructured various departments in line with specific academic plans.

We especially want to be known for the ethical component of the education we offer and for examining the role of ethics in the traditional professions as well as professional life generally. This is a university-wide effort which has been abetted by the work of a committee formed to investigate the ethical component of our curriculum and how to augment it. We are fortunate to have among our faculty some of the best known ethicists in the country, but our aim is to involve the entire faculty in providing a pervasive treatment of ethics across the curriculum.

Over the years we have established and nurtured a number of institutes and centers at Notre Dame to encourage interdisciplinary studies in areas of critical concern. These include the Kroc Institute for International Peace Studies, the Kellogg Institute for International Studies, the Center for Civil and Human Rights, our Environmental Research Center in northern Wisconsin, the Ecumenical Institute for Theological Research at Tantur in the Holy Land, and others. We want these centers and institutes to be a source of new ideas that can inform public debate and policymaking. Similar entities such as our Medieval Institute, which is among the finest in the world, perform a more traditionally scholarly function, while the Institute for Pastoral and Social Ministry, the Center for the Philosophy of Religion and the Cushwa Center for the Study of American Catholicism are vital to our role as the flagship of Catholic higher education.

The international dimension of the University, already well established, is a centerpiece of our grand strategy for the future. This dimension includes contact with individual institutions and associations of institutions in other parts of the world. In addition to our thirteen existing international studies programs in nine countries, we will continue to assess new settings for such programs. Our faculty, too, is becoming more active in international associations, as well as giving a greater international flavor to course offerings. In some instances we may establish subsidized programs in other countries for research purposes.

Peace, ecumenism, world development, the world Church: It is a large stage on which we have chosen to play, but frankly we feel we have a unique opportunity to occupy a significant role in the great dialogues of our time. Our rapid growth has positioned us for this role, our academic strength qualifies us for it, and our tradition of faith gives us a distinctive voice with which to speak. And so we shall.